MW00931968

The Complete Resource Guide for Baby Boomers

Everything You Need to Know About Caring for Your Parent

—— SECOND EDITION ——

By
Darlene Merkler
and
Elder Care Experts

The Complete Resource Guide for Baby Boomers

Everything You Need to Know About Caring for Your Parent

SECOND EDITION

Published by
Darlene Merkler
Redlands, CA

Copyright © 2019 Darlene Merkler

Cover Design by Updog Media
Interior Design by Dawn Teagarden

ISBN: 978-1-697-37525-1 (paperback)

Printed in the United States of America

First Printing: September 2019

To everyone who has been or will be a caregiver,
the families I have worked with over the past 30 years,
and the people who read through this book.

May your life be easier because of this resource guide!

Acknowledgments

DARLENE MERKLER

I want to acknowledge all of the contributing authors in this book. Every one of them is an expert in their own field, and I know how much they love seniors (and their families) and how compassionate they are about what they do. Thank you for all you do for our aging population, and thank you for taking the time to share your experience and knowledge with those who need your help now and in the future.

Thank you to UPDOG MEDIA for designing the book cover.

Thank you to my editor, Amanda Johnson (True To Intention) who has worked closely with me and each author to format the content of this book so that it would be an easy-to-read, comforting, and solution-driven book.

Contents

PART 2
Resources for Caregivers

Introduction

The Best Care for Your Loved One

ℭ𝔰

DARLENE MERKLER

If you were born between the years 1946 and 1964, then you have earned the esteemed title of "Baby Boomer" and are among the largest segment of the population in America right now. You may have just sent your last child to college or still have one or two living at home, or you may not have any children at all. You are probably still working to support yourself and loved ones in a society where two incomes are often required to pay all of the bills. And now, you are faced with what could be one of the most rewarding and difficult challenges of your life: You have the honor of taking care of one or both of the people who brought you into this world and nurtured you. You are part of the "Silver Tsunami."

If you feel alone right now, you're not. The first baby boomers reached the standard retirement of 65 in 2011. There are about 76 million boomers in the U.S., representing about 30% of the population. And 50 million people provide care for a chronically ill, disabled, or aged family member during any given year.

I have worked with families just like yours for the past thirty years and helped them make all sorts of decisions: Should Mom and Dad stay in their own home? If so, do they need in-home help? Should I place Mom and Dad in assisted living? If so, which one? How much does it cost? What if Mom can stay at home, but Dad needs to be placed? Inevitably, as I'm helping them, other questions arise: Will insurance pay for any of it? How do I enroll my other family members without conflict? Who will make all of these decisions? For these answers, I've sent them directly to the experts who have contributed to this book.

Whether you are only just becoming concerned about your parent's well-being and care or you have already been supporting them for some time, I know that you will find this book extremely helpful. The first edition of this book was published in 2009, and caregivers loved it. This second edition has all new up-to-date information from experts in their field. There are also added topics/chapters in this edition. Although some resources offer support in specific areas, this book has the answers to the most critical questions I have seen families face–in one convenient place. With the advice of the twenty contributing authors who are experts in their field, you will find just about every answer you're looking for, or you will find a name, number, or website that will lead you to a person who can help you get that answer as quickly as possible. The chapter written by the Department of Aging alone will provide you with all of the free resources and services available–resources that most people have no idea exist.

Regardless of the stage of caregiving you find yourself in, you can use this book as your step-by-step guide to lead you through this often-overwhelming honor called caregiving.

This book was designed to lift some of the burden you are feeling by helping you to address all of the major issues you are probably facing with as much knowledge and resources as possible.

Part One is meant to help you understand the basics of caregiving so that you can make the most informed decisions with or for your parent. You'll find answers to your questions about legal documents, financial planning, insurance, and home and assisted living options.

Part Two will give you access to some of the best information and resources for the elderly and their caregivers, whether it's about Alzheimer's, medications, or traveling with your parent.

Finally, and maybe most importantly, Part Three will help you to deal with some of the emotional aspects of caregiving. You'll find answers about how to support a parent through the loss of their spouse, how to resolve conflict among you and your siblings, and how to take care of yourself so that you do not end up tired, ragged, and ill yourself.

You will find that I have formatted the book as a resource guide/ workbook. Each chapter has blank pages at the end so you can track where you are with that particular subject matter, what still needs to be done, and when you will have it completed. In fact, I hope that you will use it as the primary resource for yourself and for others who may be involved in your parent's care. By putting all of the important information in one place, you will make it easier for others to support you on this journey.

May your caregiving journey be blessed!

PART 1

ʚ

Basics of Caregiving: What You Should Know

1

The Boomer's Guide to Elder Law

ଔ

JASON OEI
Elder Law Attorney

No one wants to think of their parents as getting older. After all, they raised us and took care of us. They changed our diapers, fed us, took us to school, stayed up with us when we were sick, etc. However, there will come a time when the roles will reverse–when our parents will rely on us more and more to help them through their final years with physical care and even financial matters. We will have the opportunity to repay them for the years they gave us as we take on a new role as their caregiver.

One question that you, as a new caregiver, will likely ask yourself is whether your loved ones' legal affairs are in order. Of course, this can be the one area that caregivers find confusing and intimidating. It's one thing to go with Mom or Dad to the doctor. It's a completely different thing to have to talk to a lawyer alongside them, even after you've found the right one. On top of that, you may find it difficult to talk to your elderly loved ones about their final wishes. Maybe the elder is a private individual and doesn't wish to talk about it, or maybe you fear you will come across as too nosey. The reality is, however, that it is usually a relief for everyone to have discussed your loved ones' final wishes. This is also where consulting with an attorney can be of great help.

The area of law that deals with helping individuals convey their final wishes as to the distribution of property and other related topics is called estate planning. Within estate planning, there are several further specialties. There are estate planning attorneys who specialize in what is called "elder law." Attorneys who specialize in elder law not only provide advice on estate plans, but also other areas of interest to the elderly, including long-term care planning and government benefits planning. A good elder law attorney can be an invaluable resource in navigating the legal issues unique to an aging parent.

When you look for an elder law attorney, it is always a good idea to do your research. There are several reputable attorney search engines, such as findlaw.com and avvo.com, that can help you find one in your area. In addition to finding links to the attorney's website, the search engines also include reviews from clients and colleagues. As you review the information, here are some things to consider:

1. Does the attorney belong to any legal groups that focus on estate planning or elder law?
2. What have other people said about the attorney?
3. Does the attorney have any record of discipline with their state bar association?

Finally, don't forget to ask around in your community. Your family, friends, co-workers, accountant, banker, or financial advisor may also be able to refer you to a good attorney.

Once you find the attorney, it will be time to sort through the details of your loved one's situation and wishes, as well as consider all of the possible ways to legally protect them. This chapter is meant to be a basic primer on the estate planning and elder law issues and options you will likely discuss with your attorney and then your family. Hopefully, the information in this chapter will give you enough background so that you can go into the consultation a lot more prepared and a little less nervous.

Wills and Trusts

Wills

When most people think about estate planning, they first think of a will. A will is a legal document in which a person appoints one or more individuals (sometimes called executors or personal representatives) to manage his or her estate and directs how the property in the estate is to be distributed. The property that can be governed by a will can be either real property (land, houses, etc.) or personal property (cash, jewelry, art, etc.). Once the person dies, the process of administering their will is called probate–a process whereby a court of competent jurisdiction oversees the administration of the will. Some of the things the court will do during the probate process include ensuring that the debts of the estate have been paid, that all the beneficiaries have been contacted, and that the estate property has been properly appraised. As you can imagine, the probate process can take a lot of time and it can be quite expensive, which is why most estate planning attorneys will likely recommend a trust.

Trusts

The other common estate planning document used to direct how one's property is to be distributed after death is called a trust. A trust is actually a relationship where property is held by one party for the benefit of another. The trust is established by a "trustor," who is the person setting up the trust. The trustor transfers the property to a "trustee," who is the person responsible for the care of that property. The trustee then is responsible to follow the terms of the trust, which will usually state that the property is to be used for a specific person, or the "beneficiary".

In the most common trust used in estate planning, the revocable living trust, the trustor, trustee, and beneficiary can be (and usually is) the same person. The revocable living trust will also specify what will happen to the property of the trust once the trustor passes away. The trust document should also designate at least one successor trustee–a second individual who will take responsibility for the trust should the initial trustee become incapacitated.

There are many benefits to creating a trust over a will, the most important of which I have included here:

- The use of a trust circumvents the probate process that a will would have to go through.

- The trust can be used to minimize the inheritance tax or "death tax."

- While a trust still must be administered upon the death of the trustor, the process is usually quicker and less costly than probating a will.

- A properly drafted trust can provide for divorce and creditor protection for the surviving beneficiaries.

- Finally, a properly drafted trust can also be used in conjunction with long term care and/or government benefit planning. For instance, an irrevocable trust can be an integral part of the planning to ensure that the application for benefits for either the Veterans' Administration Aid and Attendance Program or Medicaid is approved. The same trust can also be used to avoid estate recovery by the Medicaid program.

Transfer of Property During Lifetime

One method of avoiding probate, without having to do a will or a trust, is to transfer the property in question during the parents' lifetime. Usually, the property in question is the family home. For instance, the parent will add the child or children to the title of the house as joint tenants with the parent. In this example, the parent retains control of the property; but when the parent passes away, the house will go to the children through right of survivorship. While this is a perfectly acceptable solution, it is not optimal because of the adverse capital gains tax consequences to the children. Likewise, completely transferring the title of the house to the children will also have negative tax consequences. Thus, it is usually better to have a revocable living trust, just to minimize any capital gains tax consequences.

Powers of Attorney

A good estate plan will also include Powers of Attorney. Generally speaking, a Power of Attorney is a legal document where an individual (the "principal") can designate another person (the "agent") as their attorney-in-fact. Having a Power of Attorney is critical in the event that the parent loses capacity. A Power of Attorney can either be for financial matters or for healthcare decisions. We will discuss each one in turn.

Durable Power of Attorney

In a Durable Power of Attorney, the principal allows the agent to make financial decisions for them in the event that they become incapacitated. It is also always a good idea to have a second person to be the successor agent in case the first agent in not able to carry out their duties. The power to make decisions on behalf of the principal can take effect either when the principal becomes incapacitated (known as a "springing" power) or immediately upon the execution of the document. Generally, because of the delays that could be caused by the process of having to prove that the principal is in fact incapacitated, it is usually preferable to elect to have the Durable Power of Attorney effective immediately upon execution of the document.

Power of Attorney for Healthcare and Advance Healthcare Directive

In a Power of Attorney for Healthcare, the principal chooses an agent to make healthcare decisions for them in the event that they become incapacitated. For practical purposes, the agent generally should live relatively close to the principal. Also, the agent should be someone who would be comfortable communicating with medical personnel.

Within the document, there will also be room for the principal to set out their specific wishes for certain types of medical situations. This is called the Advance Healthcare Directive or Advanced Directive. It is a good idea for the principal and agent to sit down and talk about what those wishes are. For instance, does the principal want to be kept on life support in the event of a catastrophic injury where there is a very low likelihood of recovery? Does the principal have any other specific wishes relating to end of life care? As you can tell, the agent must be willing to follow the wishes of the principal, even if they have different opinions on the subject. If not, it may be better to choose a different agent.

Finally, the Power of Attorney for Healthcare should also include a HIPAA waiver. HIPAA stands for "Health Insurance Portability and Accountability Act." One of the more well-known provisions in HIPAA is that healthcare workers are required to keep patient confidentiality. This can have some unintended consequences, such as the medical staff being unable to communicate pertinent information to the relatives of someone who is receiving treatment. Having the HIPAA waiver in the Power of Attorney for Healthcare allows the agent to effectively communicate with medical staff and to find out relevant information that can assist in making medical decisions for the incapacitated principal.

Other Considerations

Conservatorship

You may be asking, "What happens if my loved one loses capacity and they have absolutely no estate planning documents in place?"

In this scenario, the documents that would have been the most useful would have been the powers of attorney. Remember, the agent under the power of attorney can act for the person who has lost capacity.

Unfortunately, in this situation, the only solution is to seek a conservatorship in court. A conservatorship is when the court appoints an individual (the "conservator") to be the responsible party for another person who does not have legal capacity (the "conservatee"). The process can be long and complicated. The legal responsibility can be for either the person, their finances, or both. The court will conduct an investigation to determine whether the proposed conservatee can care for themselves, as well as evaluate the proposed conservator to ensure that individual has the abilities to carry out the required duties. Once the conservatorship is approved, the conservator must regularly report to the court on all of their activities on behalf of the conservatee, especially financial matters. This can cause a lot of work and stress for the conservator. As you can see, a conservatorship is something that should be avoided at all costs, and an easy solution is to have properly drafted powers of attorney.

Final Thoughts

Taking care of a loved one is never easy, but you shouldn't have to worry about their legal affairs. Talking to an attorney can be a great help and give you peace of mind that the current plan covers your loved one's needs. If your loved one doesn't have an estate plan, then talking to an attorney will ensure that their legal needs will be met. Remember, planning ahead can save both you and your loved one from excess worry and stress.

Notes

2

*Making Your Loved One's
Finances Simple*

ℭℬ

MARCIA CAMPBELL
Certified Public Accountant

As seniors get older, they find managing finances a difficult task. Whether it's shaky hands, blurred vision, mood swings, or memory loss, there is usually a challenge that makes this task too frustrating and time-consuming.

The good news is that their children can ease this burden by managing finances or hiring a certified public accountant (CPA) to pay bills and monitor income.

As a CPA, I've experienced both scenarios. And they both work. It's a win-win. Let me tell you a true story:

Mr. and Mrs. E, at the time in their late eighties, lived much longer than either anticipated. It was a blessing, but they were getting tired of trying to keep track of their finances.

Their daughter knew they needed help, but she was already balancing a career and her own household, complete with husband and kids. So she hired our firm to help with Mom and Dad's financial responsibilities.

We paid Mr. and Mrs. E's regular bills and monitored their income. When they needed assistance around the house, Mr. and Mrs. E called our office, and we arranged for appropriate services.

The best part?

When Mr. and Mrs. E's daughter visited, she was able to be their (adult) child, not their financial manager. Her parents were happy, and the daughter felt reassured that they were being cared for.

I know what you're thinking: "Easier said than done with my mom (or dad)!" But that's why you're reading this chapter, right? You're here to learn the steps to financial security for seniors. Here, I will explain these challenges, placing you one decision closer to eliminating them.

First, let's discuss the option of acting as their financial manager. If your parent is alert, ask them how they want their finances managed. If you have any recommendations or reservations, let them know. This is key. Setting expectations makes the process better for everyone. Skipping this step could lead to daily spats.

As we get older, we appreciate independence. Don't take that away. If possible, allow them to take part in the revised process. Provide alternatives and simple solutions, and let them make decisions. For example, identify two banks, but let your mom or dad pick a favorite. Ask if they would like to sign checks or put you in charge of that.

These small gestures of goodwill mean everything to someone who is likely losing financial independence for the first time in more than half a century.

Of course, the process of simplifying your parent's finances could lead to revising bank account systems. If your loved one resists, consider hiring a third party for support.

Don't forget: Working with your parent now decreases the number of tough financial decisions after he/she passes.

Bank Accounts

Make sure all income is automatically deposited, including pensions, Social Security, and brokerage income. Pay debts through online bill pay or automatic withdrawal. This prevents checks or bills getting lost in stacks of paper.

Review bank statements regularly to guard against unauthorized withdrawals and identify theft. Keep balances under FDIC limits.

Unfortunately, elderly people whose bodies and minds are failing are easy targets for thieves.

Also, make sure the type of bank account suits your parent's needs. Some banks charge a monthly fee if the balance drops under a certain amount.

Pension Plans/IRAs

Combine plans when possible. If your parent is over 70½, take out Required Minimum Distributions. Review any pension plan to confirm the beneficiary. Often, parents tell us who they think is the beneficiary, yet the document lists a different person.

Debt

While reviewing bank statements, search for mortgage payments, credit card payments, and unusual payments made via check. According to the 2004 Survey of Consumer Finances, issued by the Federal Reserve Board, Americans ages 65 to 74 spend nearly 75% of their annual income on debt payments.

If you find debt, find the cause. Can your parent afford this necessity on a fixed income? Is your mom or dad overspending on non-essentials?

Visit https://www.annualcreditreport.com to order free credit reports from all three credit report companies. Review these documents regularly in search of debt and potential identity theft.

Benefits

Make sure your mom and dad receive any entitled benefits. Visit http://www.benefitscheckup.org. This site helps older Americans discover federal and state assistance programs.

Tax Returns

Most seniors find taxes confusing, even frustrating. (And you thought you had nothing in common with your aging parents!)

When did your mom or dad last file a tax return? Find out. Penalties and interest add up quickly. If income is low, your parent may not meet filing requirements. Ask anyway.

Opt for e-file tax returns. That way, tax refunds, tax liabilities, and estimate payments can be deposited and/or withdrawn automatically.

Credit cards can accumulate deductible expenses for tax returns, and some companies offer lists of yearly expenses in different categories. Brokerage houses also offer similar statements. Pharmacies give prescription lists. All of these resources keep your parent's finances ready for tax season.

Note: Under certain circumstances, the cost of living in a facility or hiring help at home may qualify as a medical deduction.

Insurance Policies

Gather all policies in need of review. Make sure beneficiaries are current and not a divorced or deceased spouse.

Are premiums being paid, or are these "paid up" policies? Depending on your answer, these policies may be an untapped source of income. Consider hiring a qualified insurance evaluator to review the viability of the policies.

Trusts

Confirm that trust documents are accurate, including current health directives for medical decisions. If there is a trust, make sure your parent's assets have the correct titles, including real estate holdings. Review the beneficiaries of the trust and confirm they are not deceased or fallen out of favor with your parent. Not sure? Allow an attorney to review the documents.

If one of your parents has died, review the trust to make sure assets are distributed correctly. Confirm that tax filings are completed, including fiduciary tax returns (Form 1041) and estate tax returns (Form 706), if applicable.

Mail/Phone

Consider forwarding mail related to income and expenses to your address. This tactic ensures important documents will not be lost.

As your parents age, they may need help sorting through mail, including magazines, catalogs, and donation requests. They may not distinguish junk mail from important documents, so sit down with them to check mail, especially items that involve purchase or donation options.

Also, add your parent's phone number to the Do Not Call Registry to protect them from high-pressure sales and identity thieves.

Unclaimed Property

All states operate websites that allow you to search for unclaimed cash or property. Years ago, did mom or dad live in a different state?

Search in your parent's current state, as well as states he/she previously lived in. You may find small bank accounts, forgotten long ago, along with interest and dividends that were never claimed.

Your parents may own stock in a brokerage account. They also could have owned separate shares of stock that were held outside of the brokerage account. Years ago, some mutual companies that became stock companies sent stock shares and dividends to policy holders. Did your parent own one of these polices? Check the state's unclaimed property section for these also.

Dementia/Stroke

It's challenging to communicate with loved ones suffering from memory loss or other health issues. Because of this, you may not get involved in your mom or dad's financial matters until years later, and this would be a mistake. Get ready to discover checks that were never deposited, past due notices, and missing paperwork.

If this is what your family is facing, start with checking bank accounts and credit reports. Then, follow the steps listed above.

Work with an attorney to file power of attorney or other legal documents. You may have to obtain legal documents to speak on your parent's behalf.

A Third Party

Helping elderly parents can be challenging. In many cases, Mom or Dad is not mentally or physically able to help. In other cases, they resist assistance.

Consider hiring a neutral third party such as a CPA or a private fiduciary. Remember, it's important to work with advisors that you and your parents approve and that will work as a team together for your parent.

Conclusion

Helping mom or dad with finances brings plenty of emotions to the surface. You, as the child, may consider your parent mentally feeble. You may believe you are better prepared to handle you mom or dad's affairs. You just want to take control and "fix it." Meanwhile, they may not want to relinquish control to one of their children. No matter how old you are, you're still their child, or they don't want to relinquish their independence or privacy to anybody. They may be short-tempered, and they may refuse to work with you.

This situation can add stress to the lives of everybody involved.

Remember, this is all normal. Do not take any of it personally. Your loved one is upset with the situation, not necessarily with you. They feel helpless. If you're lucky, you may live long enough to experience this, too.

How do you deal with these emotions? I'll tell you.

Listen (a lot!). If you let your parent express his/her opinions, you may discover nuggets of important information!

For instance, you're thinking about hiring a caretaker. You believe you've found the right person, but you mom or dad keeps mentioning "Debbie." They probably want you to hire Debbie, so maybe you should take a second look at her resume.

Don't force your choice on your parent. It's the same advice I gave earlier about choosing banks. Empower your parent by offering vetted choices.

Finally, remember that you can hire a third party to work through any problems.

Questions to Help

- Is my loved one alert and willing to work with me, or a third party?

- Are they suffering from health issues or memory loss that will require me to become a legal advocate for them?

- Do I have easy access to their financial paperwork, or do I have to search?

- Am I okay with wearing multiple hats– daughter/son and financial manager–or would I prefer to hire professional assistance?

- Have I asked my loved one what they really want?

- Do I understand what they want, or am I trying to tell them what to do?

- Do I need to bring in a third-party CPA or attorney to assist?

- Do I have a list of all of the bank accounts, brokerage accounts, IRAs and pension plans, and insurance policies that my parent has?

- Do I have a list of all of the credit cards, loans, and everyday bills that my parent pays?

- Do I have a list of all of the advisors that my parents use along with their contact information?

Handy Websites

Do Not Call Registry (land lines and cell phones):
visit www.DoNotCall.gov or call 888.382.1222

Claim lost money or property at state controller's office.
Each state has a website. Here is the website for California:
https://sco.ca.gov/upd_msg.html

Veterans Administration's Aid and Attendance Program:
https://www.benefits.va.gov/pension/aid_attendance_
housebound.asp

CTAP: www.ddtp.org. Provides free phones for hearing
impaired/disabled persons in California.

Benefits Checkup: www.benefitscheckup.org

Social Security: www.ssa.gov

Receive benefits sooner than later: www.socialsecurity.gov/
OACT/quickcalc/early_late.html

For answers to frequently asked questions about Social Security,
visit: www.ncpssm.org/contact/ask/

Marcia L. Campbell, CPA, CSA, AEP
A Professional Corporation
Financial Services for Elderly Clients:

- Supervising household expenditures
- Accounting for income and payment of bills
- Tax preparation and planning
- Estate planning consulting
- Accounting for estates and trusts
- Financial power of attorney
- Private fiduciary services
- Court and trust accountings

Marcia has more than twenty-five years of experience as a Certified Public Accountant (CPA). Her experience includes tax planning and preparation of individual, and fiduciary tax returns. She assists clients with estate and financial planning.

In addition, Marcia is a Professional Fiduciary and provides services to trusts in the capacity of trustee. Services include asset gathering, bill paying and review of legal documents, beneficiary designations and titles of assets. She also prepares court and trust accountings done the way the probate court requires them to be done. She also acts as a trustee for life insurance trusts utilized in estate planning.

1313 Chicago Avenue, Suite 200
Riverside, CA 92507

Phone: (951) 686-3608 Fax: (951) 686-3304

www.MCampbellCPA.com

E-mail: Marcia@MCampbellCPA.com

Notes

3

*Insurance Options to Protect
Your Assets and Family*

‍ଔ

LUKE KIBLER
Vantage Insurance Solutions

We live in a day and time when information travels around the world and back in no time flat, and it sometimes seems that misinformation travels even more speedily. Going online, you can research any subject and, in seconds, have an overwhelming number of opinions, commentary, and analytics from all over the globe. They will express opposing views, absurd excuses for logic, and dizzyingly complex paths of reasoning. I bring this up from the start because the subject we are going to dive into here is a classic source of incredible debate and misinformation. As I advise clients from all walks of life, I find it startling how misinformed many are, and how they have been programmed by clever marketing and popular culture to focus on and believe things that are untrue or irrelevant. I find that sometimes it isn't ignorance, but rather the illusion of knowledge, that is the biggest obstacle to moving in the right direction and making a significant change to one's thinking, habits, and financial future.

My goal in this brief chapter is to bring simplicity and clarity to a complex subject. I hope to help you cut through the noise of passionate sales people and self-proclaimed gurus and get some real down-and-dirty facts about your best options for protecting your family and wealth today, using strategically-designed and purchased insurance products. So let's dive right in!

Option #1–The Art of Procrastination (AKA, The Ostrich Technique)

This "#1" option is not #1 because it is the most effective, most profitable, or overall best option to implement. It's #1 because it's the most popular. Here's how it works: Simply go about your life, work, and recreation as if nothing is ever going change or happen. Pretend you're going to live forever, never get sick or injured, and never have financial challenges. And... voila! You're done. That was easy, right? Enjoy that feeling because that's the end of the "good" that comes from this bury-your-head-in-the-sand "strategy." This wildly popular option is wreaking havoc all throughout our society. Millions of people enter their final years of life unprepared and positioned for financial and emotional ruin. Stripped of their dignity, they are forced to upend their loved ones' lives and depend on them daily. While this first option is the most popular and the easiest (initially) to "implement," it is also the most costly and stressful in the end.

All too often, I talk with people I meet in the community, or with new clients, that say something along the lines of, "Where were you twenty years ago?! I sure wish I had heard about these options then." It's true that it would have been much better to start your planning and buying of the right protection long ago. However, that's no reason to not start making wise choices right now. Let's be honest, we are creatures of habit, aren't we? We resist change. We tend to do the easiest and most pleasant things first, and the most difficult (and often most important) things last–if we get to them at all. But time is our most valuable asset! Your life insurance or long-term care insurance coverage will likely never be as cost-efficient, or even profitable, as it is right now. The time to make important things a priority and take action is now.

Often, well-meaning people tell me they just plan to work until they die, or that their children will just take care of them and they don't need to worry about it. Here's some truth for you: You don't get to choose when you die. You don't get to choose how (except for one way that no one would recommend). You don't really get to choose if your mind and body remains healthy and vibrant to the end. I'm going to ask you to stop and imagine something right now. I want you to imagine you've just gotten the news that through deteriorating health, or an injury, you suddenly find yourself unable to take care of some of your most basic needs.

Your doctor just confirmed to you that your condition is permanent and progressive. Do you really *want* to ask your children to quit their career, change how they might be raising their own children, and set aside just about all they are doing in life right now, to get you dressed every day, clean your messes, and bathe you? Do you really want to put major strain on your family's finances and lives? You suddenly realize your savings will be exhausted within just a couple years if you pay for care elsewhere. You are stuck. How do you feel? You have no good options. The sinking feeling in your stomach tightens into a painful knot of deep sadness and regret as you realize how simple things could have been had you planned ahead. Is this going to be your story? It's up to you. One of the biggest reasons for planning how you will finance the costs of long-term care is to preserve your dignity, and that of the ones you love, so that you are able to spend your final days interacting with your family in the best ways possible. Listen, we all will one day grow old and die. It's true. Why deny it? Why treat discussing it and planning for it like it's taboo or bad luck? This is one of those things that doesn't just go away if you ignore it. So, let's talk options. Let's face it, deal with it, plan for it, and enjoy our lives like we are meant to!

Here are some of the facts and statistics to help drive this point home—the numbers on the realities surrounding long term care are pretty daunting:

According to recent stats[1], 7 out of every 10 people 65 and older will need long term care.

According to one of the leading long-term care insurance providers in the country, over 59% of long-term care claims last more than

---

[1] 2017 U.S. Department of Health and Human Services 10/10/2017.

one year, and of those, the average length of time care is needed is 4.2 years.

The California median cost for home care is $57,204 per year. The average cost of nursing home care is $97,368 for a "semi-private room" and $116,436 for a private room.[2]

Few circumstances in life will utterly drain your assets like paying for good long-term care. As the old saying goes, the question isn't "can you afford to buy a policy or plan?" because you can't afford *not to* put a plan into effect. So what are your options? Well, you may be surprised to find that you have more than you realize. Now that we agree that this first "strategy" of ostrich imitation is not the default decision you want to make, let's move on. Here's a quick summary of the top options you should consider, along with some pros and cons to help you narrow down what makes the most sense for you.

Long Term Care Insurance–The Pure Approach

This is the most straightforward method for purchasing protection against the devastating costs of extended health care, or long-term care. In a certain sense, it will almost always give you the highest benefit limit for your dollars in long-term care benefits. You might also find this option to be more affordable than you think. It is based on providing a set "cost per day" benefit, for a certain number of years. For example, $250 per day, for 36 months, or 3 years. Another key factor that affects your premiums is your choice of "elimination period." Think of it like a time deductible. You can typically choose from 30 days to 120 days, and sometimes more. During this time, you are responsible for your costs. Once the elimination period is met, your benefit payments kick in.

---

[2] Genworth cost of care survey, 2017

These plans pay based on what's called a "reimbursement basis," not in advance. In other words, even if your benefit limit adds up to $8,000 per month, if your actual costs for care are $4,700, that is what is reimbursed. Also, this means you may be required to pay the costs of care initially, and then will be sent reimbursement payments from the insurance company so your cost is zero. And don't worry, many carriers now work directly with your care providers, whether in-home or in a facility, and provide direct payment to them rather than you having to pay out-of-pocket on the cost and wait (with nervous trepidation) to get paid back.

The primary downside that people see in this product is this: If they die without needing care, then the money spent on this insurance is "lost". It has one purpose, and is purely protection, just like your auto insurance or home owner's insurance. One more thing worth noting: Premiums are not guaranteed. While a change in rates is uncommon, if they do change, it's usually an increase. This unknown can also be unsettling. Is it still a worthwhile purchase? Absolutely. The bottom line is, you are still able to receive back in coverage for care dramatically more than the dollars you paid in premium, especially if you end up needing care only a few years into buying the policy.

Life Insurance–A Relevant and Powerful Tool for All Seasons of Life

Life insurance might be one of the most misunderstood and under-utilized financial instruments among the middle class. I would venture to say that the majority of people, even many of those in the financial industry that sell these products for a living, don't understand its uses beyond simple premature death protection and covering specific debts or final expenses. It's unfortunate, because life insurance, properly designed, can be used as a powerful tax-free wealth accumulation tool, wealth transfer tool, retirement tool, and much more. If your insurance agent doesn't do more than "quote" you prices on life insurance, I would recommend that you fire them and find someone that genuinely specializes in the uses of life insurance for wealth planning.

Getting back to our theme of planning and protection for the final stages of life, you need to know that in this day and age, you have most life insurance carriers in California that offer a variety of "living benefits," also known as "ABRs" or Accelerated Benefit Riders. These riders allow you to use your death benefit, while still living, for a variety of health conditions and even injuries. Several carriers offer a life insurance product with one such rider, typically called a "Chronic Illness Rider," that will allow you to use some of your death benefit to pay for long-term-care-type expenses. Most life insurance policies only allow you to use a percentage, typically 50%, but there are certain policies that allow up to even 100%. The benefit is triggered by the same thing as long-term care insurance– loss of 2 ADLs (activities of daily living) or mental illness. This can be a very cost-efficient way to cover your bases, and get your dollars multi-tasking, which I strongly believe to be a key principle in wealth accumulation and protection. It is also another reason why you would never want to allow a properly-designed life insurance policy to lapse or simply end because the term is up. It could cost you and your family hundreds of thousands of lost dollars in medical expenses that could have been paid out by your life insurance. Even if you have significant wealth, this is just smart planning and good math.

Some potential downsides would be that you may not get as great a benefit amount for LTC protection as a straight LTC policy would provide. Also, you need to remember that if you use some or most of your death benefit for long-term care needs, this directly reduces the life insurance benefit paid to your beneficiaries. Lastly, it's noteworthy to point out that life insurance policies typically pay out benefits like this differently than long-term care policies. Rather than the reimbursement model mentioned earlier, they use a method called "Indemnity." This means that you can receive the full amount of your benefit limit that you are eligible for, should you desire, regardless of your actual costs. This money can then be spent however you see fit–a nice Caribbean cruise, a trip to the French Riviera, that sports car you've always wanted, or a ticket on the next Mars expedition!

Long-Term Care Annuities & Hybrid Whole Life Policies
This is one of the newer options, and one of my personal favorites. These products are very flexible in how they can be funded, designed, and paid out. You can pay for a product like this with all the typical modes with after-tax money: monthly, quarterly, semi-annually, and annually. Also, as a qualified annuity version, you can fund it with a rollover, known as a 1035 exchange, of qualified funds from an IRA, 401k, or similar tax-deferred retirement accounts. This means, you could roll money straight out of an IRA or 401k and into one of these without creating a taxable event. So, if you have funds wasting away in a retirement account somewhere, this might be a really good option for a portion of those funds. Another nice thing to note is that much like their life insurance-based counterparts, they build cash value and earn guaranteed interest!

In short, these products can give you great peace of mind knowing that no matter what happens, you get to "have it all." Should you need long-term care, like most people, the dollars spent on this product will buy far more in benefits than the dollars themselves would ever provide. Should you die suddenly, without needing care, the entire benefit pool pays out like normal life insurance to your beneficiaries. And, should you live longer and healthier than you expected, and need some of that money back out, the principle is liquid, guaranteed, and will also be credited with a typical 3-4% interest earnings annually. Pretty snazzy, huh?

Again, like anything, there are trade-offs. The main downside here would be that you will get more long-term care benefits for your dollars when you purchase pure long-term care insurance, as opposed to a hybrid like this. Also, you would get more life insurance for your dollars if you purchase a pure life insurance product. However, I should also mention, these products also have the option to purchase a "Continuation of Benefits Rider" that will either double your payout, or continue to pay out up to maximum monthly plan benefits without limit.

There is much more that could be said on the subject as relates to plan design options, carrier comparisons, and the many unique tax benefits, but alas–we are out of time. So hopefully you have some good food for thought, and it's my sincere desire that you can find renewed hope, vigor, and clarity to make up your mind to get your planning and preparing done, and your insurance protection in force, like you have been meaning to for years. It will never be cheaper than it is today, and if you are already in your 50s, 60s, or older, chances are you are also about as healthy as you will ever be. Waiting only costs you more, and potentially could cost you the ability to even have a choice, should an unexpected illness or injury render you uninsurable. Getting valuable protection like this can be much more affordable than you think, and you will rest much easier knowing it is in place–securing your future, protecting your loved ones and your assets, and helping you leave a legacy that gives you a deep sense of pride and joy.

Questions:

1. What stood out to you or impacted you the most in this chapter?

2. What plans and preparations have you already made?

3. Do you feel these plans are up to date and sufficient in every way? If not, list out what you think is missing right now.

4. What are your top questions you need to seek answers to right away?

5. What top priorities do you see need to be addressed and dealt with?

6. What immediate action steps do you intend to take? List out your top 3 at minimum.

7. What are your desires for...?

    7.1 Long-term care: Where do you want to receive care? How do you want to pay for it? Who do you want handling your affairs when you are no longer able?

    7.2 Funeral and final affairs. (And what are the associated costs?)

    7.3 Inheritance to children and/or grandchildren.

    7.4 Charitable giving.

Notes

4

*Medi-Cal: How to Fund
Your Loved One's Care*

☙

ESTHER WANG
Elder Law Attorney

A ccording to one study, more than sixty-eight percent of the elderly population in the U.S. will require nursing home care before they die. Patients who experience sudden illnesses, such as strokes and injuries caused by accidents, often require rehabilitations in skilled nursing homes after hospital stays. An Alzheimer's patient's long-term care cost during his or her lifetime is approximately $190,000. And, in California, a skilled nursing facility often charges more than $8,000 per month per patient. Thus, most patients and their families need to turn to public benefit programs for assistance.

There are many long-term care services provided for Medi-Cal recipients. In addition to rehabilitation care and long-term care in a skilled nursing facility, California's In-Home Supportive Services program (IHSS) provides personal care assistance to eligible Medi-Cal recipients who need home care services. Many counties offer PACE, or Program of All-Inclusive Care for Elderly, which helps pay for elderly daycare services, home care services, and assisted living facilities. The Assisted Living Waiver Program offers assisted living care for eligible Medi-Cal recipients.

Is It Legal for People with Assets to Qualify for Medi-Cal Benefit?

This is a question most frequently asked by people who have assets but are faced with the enormous long-term care cost and wish to avail themselves to Medi-Cal benefit. Medi-Cal planning, like income tax planning, is 100% legal; and the better you plan, the more money you will save.

Medicaid is called Medi-Cal in California. You are not alone if you are perplexed by Medi-Cal laws. The courts feel the same way. According to the U.S. Supreme Court, the Medicaid Act is "an aggravated assault on the English language, resistant to attempts to understand it." A circuit court described the Medicaid Act as one of the "most completely impenetrable texts within human experience" and "dense reading of the most tortuous kind." Yet another judge commented: "The Medicaid Act is actually a morass of interconnecting legislation. It contains provisions which are circuitous and, at best, difficult to harmonize." Yet, once you receive proper advice and know how to use Medi-Cal law to your financial advantage, it can help you protect your hard-earned assets and provide long-term care for you and your loved ones.

Medi-Cal planning can be done for a simple estate or a complicated one. We know from experience that we can obtain Medi-Cal benefit for a married couple who owns eleven rental properties or another person who has more than $1 million in liquid assets. These are not isolated cases. They can be executed because the rules were followed very carefully.

It is important to know that there are different types of Medi-Cal benefits and the laws and legal strategies described here do not apply to all types of Medi-Cal benefits, but only to the long-term care benefit. Please also be advised that unless you have no assets, it is important to consult with an elder law attorney for Medi-Cal planning.

Asset v. Income

In order to understand Medi-Cal rules, please understand that Medi-Cal treats assets and income differently. For eligibility purposes, Medi-Cal applies limitations and transfers to assets only; and your eligibility will be determined by the value of your assets, not your income. Your income will be important in determining your share of cost, which will be discussed later, but not for eligibility purposes.

Typically, monies that are received monthly are income. Monthly social security benefits, pensions, rental and interest income are examples of income. Monthly annuities are income. Earned income, such as wages, is also income, although we don't usually find our elderly clients with earned income.

Assets include, but are not limited to, primary residences, rental properties, and investment and bank accounts. Income that is not spent or gifted during the month it is received becomes an asset for the following month. Inheritances received in a given month are considered income for that month and, if not spent down, become assets the following month.

Exempt Assets v. Non-Exempt Assets
Once a resource is determined to be an asset, the next step is to determine whether it is an exempt or non-exempt asset. In planning, it is important to identify all of your exempt assets. Once all exempt assets are identified, the rest are non-exempt assets.

Exempt assets include:
1. Your primary residence;
2. One vehicle;
3. All household items and personal effects;
4. Life insurance policy with a surrender value of $1500 or less;
5. Musical instruments;
6. Business assets; and
7. Self-supporting assets.

Non-exempt assets include:
1. Bank accounts and investment accounts;

2. Retirement accounts, such as IRA and 401 (k) accounts;

3. Rental properties;

4. Annuities; and

5. Vehicles (other than the first one).

You can have all of the exempt assets and qualify for Medi-Cal benefit. Thus, one legal strategy is to convert the non-exempt assets to exempt assets. For example, rental properties, while they are not primary residence, can be classified as a business asset because they generate income and provide support to the person applying for Medi-Cal benefit. Likewise, retirement accounts can be considered exempt assets if they have regular distributions and therefore are self-supporting assets, which are exempt. These are just some of the examples of how the laws can be utilized to benefit a person who needs to obtain Medi-Cal benefit.

Single Person: If you are a single person, you can keep all exempt assets and up to $2000 in non-exempt assets and qualify for Medi-Cal benefit.

Married Couple: If you are a married couple, you can keep all exempt assets, and then divide the non-exempt assets cleverly. The spouse that requires long-term care (and therefore the one that wants Medi-Cal benefit) can have no more than $2000 of non-exempt assets, and the spouse that does not need Medi-Cal benefit can keep up to $126,420 in non-exempt assets (this figure is as of June, 2019). The non-exempt assets, up to $126,420, that can be kept by the healthy spouse are called the Community Spouse Resource Allowance, or CSRA. A married couple will be able to keep more assets because of California Spousal Protection Law.

Income and Share of Cost

While your income does not determine whether you can be eligible for Medi-Cal benefit, it does determine how much you will pay as your "share of cost." Share of cost is like a co-pay for Medi-Cal, which is your share of the medical expenses that you need to pay on a monthly basis. Share of cost is calculated differently depending on what Medi-Cal services are needed.

For example, if you need skilled nursing care, the share of cost for a single person will be your entire income minus $35. Yet if you are a married couple, with a few exceptions, the share of cost will be the entire combined income of you and your spouse minus $3,161 (minimum monthly maintenance needs allowance, or MMMNA). This figure is updated annually.

If you need PACE services for home care, it depends on the provider under PACE. For example, currently, for the provider in San Bernardino County and Riverside County, there is no share of cost for home care services, but the share of cost for assisted living care is your income minus $134.

If you have rental properties, it is possible to shift the rental income to an irrevocable trust so that the income would not be subject to the share of cost.

Transfer Rules and Look-Back under Medi-Cal

When you apply for Medi-Cal long-term care coverage, Medi-Cal conducts a review, or "look-back," to determine whether you or your spouse transferred assets (e.g. cash gifts, home ownership, etc.) to another person or party for less than fair market value. When you transfer assets for less than fair market value, the transfers are subject to a penalty that delays the date you can qualify to receive Medi-Cal long-term care services.

Currently, California follows a law that uses a 30-month look-back period for most transfers, except for transfers to a revocable trust. This means that Medi-Cal does not make inquiry of transfers which occurred earlier than 30 months prior to the month of the application of Medi-Cal long-term care benefit, including nursing home benefits.

Legal Strategies to Become Eligible for Medi-Cal Benefit

While there are many more strategies than referenced here, these are some of the examples of Medi-Cal planning:

1. Converting Non-Exempt Assets to Exempt Assets: An example of this would be to convert a rental property, which is non-exempt (because it is not a primary residence), to an exempt business asset or exempt self-supporting asset.

2. Gift Assets and Wait It Out: This planning strategy works if long-term care is anticipated "down the road." the elderly parent may consider giving his/her assets to the children or intended heirs of the estate and just wait out the penalized period or the look-back period.

3. Enlargement of the CSRA and MMMNA: Let's say that a couple has non-exempt assets over the CSRA, or over $126,420, and we would like the healthy spouse to be able to keep all of the joint assets of $400,000. We can file a petition with the Superior Court under Probate Code sections 3100 to 3154. Probate Code sections 3100 to 3154 allow the court to authorize a proposed transaction involving spouses if (1) one spouse lacks the legal capacity for the proposed transaction or has a conservator and (2) the other spouse has legal capacity or has a conservator. When the petition is granted, then the healthy spouse will

be able to keep the assets in his or her name or trust and still qualify the ill spouse for Medi-Cal benefit.

Estate Recovery

"Estate recovery" refers to the law that mandates California to take the properties of Medi-Cal recipients to pay for the cost incurred by the state for the Medi-Cal recipients. This law causes many people to fear the loss of their homes, but estate recovery can be completely avoided with proper planning. You don't need to lose your asses to the state if the assets, including a home, are in a revocable living trust or irrevocable living trust, or if you have a surviving spouse at the time you die, or if you are survived by a child who is on social security disability.

Common Medi-Cal Mistakes

Over the years, we have seen a lot of people made mistakes because they lack proper guidance. Here are some examples:

1. **Cashing Out the Retirement Accounts:** Some people believe that they need to cash out their retirement accounts in order to qualify for Medi-Cal benefit. That is not true. While a retirement account is a non-exempt asset, you don't need to cash it out. You only need to convert it to an exempt asset by taking a monthly distribution, making the retirement account now an exempt asset. Cashing out your retirement account will have tax consequences, as the amount cashed out will be considered income and you will need to pay taxes on that income.

2. **Giving the House to the Children by a Deed:** In our experience, this is the most serious mistake made by people. To avoid estate recovery, they either transfer the house to their children or put their children's names on the deed as joint tenants with the right of survivorship. While

it is true that by doing so you can avoid estate recovery, it often creates irreversible income tax consequence when the parent (on Medi-Cal) dies. The best way to transfer a house to a child (or children) is by either a revocable living trust or irrevocable living trust, because there will be no negative tax consequence and you will still be able to avoid estate recovery.

3. **Hiding Money and Not Reporting this to Medi-Cal at the Time of the Application:** It is a criminal act to do this, so don't do it. An experienced elder law attorney can help you navigate the rules. You never have to commit fraud in order to obtain Medi-Cal benefit.

For people without much assets, obtaining Medi-Cal benefit involves time and effort. For people with assets that wish to obtain Medi-Cal benefit, it also takes legal expertise. It will be worth your while to discuss your specific situation with an experienced elder law attorney.

Notes

_____

_____

_____

_____

_____

_____

_____

_____

_____

_____

_____

_____

_____

_____

_____

_____

_____

Notes

5

Understanding Medicare

☙

HICAP

Is Medicare really mysterious and complex? It's not called the "Medicare Maze" for nothing! Actually, it's crucial to understand all parts of Medicare in order to *maximize* its benefits and get them to fit a person's lifestyle. I have been explaining Medicare for almost seventeen years, and I still don't understand it completely. There are a number of reasons for the confusion: 1) it changes frequently, 2) rules exist for each and every situation, and 3) only the common situations happen often.

Eligibility for Medicare

Those eligible for Medicare Part A fall into one or more of the following categories:

- People who have reached their sixty-fifth birthday and who have worked and paid Medicare taxes for forty quarters or more OR who are married to someone who has fulfilled that requirement for them will be automatically eligible for Medicare's Part A at no cost. They will also be offered Part B at that time.

- Legal immigrants who are sixty-five or older and have been in the country for five years or more may also be eligible for Medicare coverage.

- Disabled people who have worked for twenty quarters or more may also be eligible for Medicare if they are permanently unable to work. They must wait until they have received their twenty-fifth Social Security Disability check before their Medicare coverage is effective. Advocates are currently attempting to get Congress to remove that waiting period, citing the many disabled beneficiaries who die before their health care benefits start.

You can apply for Part B at your local Social Security office or by going online. Part B is a "voluntary" benefit with a set charge, which may vary depending upon your taxable income and whether you are married.

Failure to enroll in Part B when you are first eligible may trigger a penalty if you change your mind and enroll later (unless you continue to work and are covered by an employer plan).

Initially, a person can start Medicare coverage in relation to their sixty-fifth birthday or when they are scheduled to receive the twenty-fifth Social Security Disability check. It can begin at any time during the calendar year. After the initial enrollment, changes usually can be made only at certain times of the year. For example, if you do not accept Part B (maybe because you don't want to pay the premium), you can later change your mind. Then you will have to apply for Part B during the first three months of the calendar year. Benefits will not begin until July 1st of that year – possibly a long wait to get treatment and have coverage for those bills! You will most likely be assessed a penalty for each year you were not signed up for Part B and could have been. This premium increase is permanent. If you think your situation is exceptional, you can appeal to Social Security.

Part A – What Is and What Is NOT Covered

Part A is usually referred to as "hospitalization coverage." This phrase is correct but incomplete. There is the obvious coverage for inpatient care in regular acute care hospitals.

Medicare also covers:

- Skilled care in inpatient rehabilitation facilities
- Skilled nursing facilities (nursing homes)
- Hospice programs
- Home health care services
- Care in certain religious non-medical health care institutions

Call Medicare if you need more information about any of these types of care.

Medicare has rules and restrictions for coverage in each of these situations. The most common of these is that the care being given (and required by the doctors' orders) must be SKILLED care – requiring the services of a licensed doctor, nurse, or therapist. When you require skilled care, you also have coverage for the custodial care that goes with it to take care of you (meals, laundry, bathing, etc.). Once you no longer require skilled care, your eligibility for Medicare coverage usually stops. Generally, covered benefits in a hospital include a semi-private room and drugs as part of inpatient treatment, as well as necessary supplies and general nursing.

Part A, however, does NOT cover:

- Private rooms in a hospital unless they are medically necessary
- Comfort items, such as a phone or TV
- Personal care items, like a razor or shampoo
- Acupuncture
- Dental surgery (even when done in a hospital)
- Emergency room care

- Cosmetic surgery
- Most surgical procedures performed in ambulatory surgical centers

Part B – What Is and What Is NOT Covered

Part B is known as "Medical or Outpatient Insurance." Sometimes people who see this phrase on their Medicare card *incorrectly* assume they have Medi-Cal benefits!

Part B covers doctors' services, outpatient care, and limited preventive services. Part B (like Part A) services must be medically necessary, meet medical practice standards, and be performed by Medicare providers. Part B services are extensive.

Some examples of coverage are:

- Ambulance services
- Blood services (limitations apply)
- Clinical lab services
- Very limited chiropractic services
- Clinical research studies
- Preventive diagnostic screenings
- Defibrillator implantation
- Diabetes self-management training and supplies (not including insulin and syringes)
- Doctors' services
- Durable medical equipment
- Emergency room services
- Injections, including preventive shots
- Foot exams and care (if prescribed)

- Home health care
- Kidney dialysis and supplies
- Outpatient mental health care
- Outpatient occupational and physical therapy
- Prosthetic and orthotic items
- Second surgical opinions

After reading this partial list, you certainly must understand the necessity of having Part B coverage!

What, then, is NOT covered by Part B?

- Acupuncture
- Ambulance services, except for emergency situations
- Most chiropractic services
- Custodial care by itself
- Dental care of all kinds
- Dentures
- Routine eye exams (except for eye diseases)
- Eyeglasses (unless prescribed after cataract surgery)
- Routine foot care (except for diabetics)
- Hearing aids and exams
- Hearing tests unless ordered by your doctor
- Some lab tests
- Orthopedic shoes (limited)
- Routine physical exams
- Most prescription drugs
- Insulin if used with a pump only

- Medical equipment for personal convenience
- Routine medical care when traveling outside the United States

Part C – Medicare Advantage Plans – How Do They Work and How Are They Different from Medicare?

Originally, Medicare made contracts with private insurance companies. They are known as health maintenance organizations (HMOs). These arrangements offer comprehensive healthcare to beneficiaries at a cost lower than what Medicare would charge.

Medicare has a yearly deductible for health services which must be paid out of pocket before Medicare's coverage starts for the year. Medicare also only pays for 80% of most covered services. A patient who has had a lot of medical procedures during the year would need to pay a great amount of money for the uncovered 20%. Consequently, those who can afford (and want to) can buy a private supplemental insurance plan – commonly known as a "Medi-Gap." This plan pays for the difference between what Medicare pays and the remaining allowed cost. Medicare standardized the Medi-Gap plans in 1992 to provide a range of benefits, from the most basic (and least expensive) to those that would cover extra care (such as preventive tests) and even half the cost of prescriptions (before Part D came along).

HMO plans were designed to eliminate the need for supplemental insurance and separate drug plans. Beneficiaries are required to pay small "co-pays" for office visits, lab fees, reduced drug costs, and monthly premiums. Since there is no deductible, coverage starts immediately. Medicare pre-pays a fee to the HMO each month for every patient signed up with their plan. The fees vary by the overall cost of medical care in the area where the beneficiaries live. HMO plans may not cover remote or rural areas. All members of the plans have to go to plan-contracted local doctors, medical groups, and hospitals. Only emergency care is available to members outside of the local area.

Medicare and HMOs differ in the way payment is received for care. HMOs receive a pre-set amount each month from Medicare for every person signed up with the plan, whether or not the patient uses the plan that month. Medicare and most private insurance, in contrast, set a fee for the specific medical care that has been done for the patient after it has been completed. This is the difference between pre-paid and fee for service. The difference in the payment method is the result in HMOs' attempts to keep medical costs down. This also includes preventive screenings and tests which could result in early detection of chronic conditions, fewer emergency situations, and overall better healthcare. Medicare, which receives its payment only when a patient needs care, tends to perform more and more exploratory tests and procedures in response to patient-reported pain and other symptoms. Over time, however, Medicare (which still bills on a fee-for-service basis) has generally adopted the managed care practice of preventive care testing and screenings at various ages and times.

As years passed, many insurance companies began to offer managed care and tried different types of arrangements. Another type of plan, the Preferred Provider Organization (PPO), has been around for many years, as a private plan, an employer group plan, and as a type of Medicare managed care. It seems to work well in any of those payment arrangements because it is flexible. The only difference is who is paying for it and what the rate is. A PPO allows the subscriber greater choice in where the patient gets healthcare and from whom. Generally, the member pays a monthly fee or premium whether he requires use of the plan that month or not. Like the HMO, if he or she requires doctors' services, there would be a small co-pay as long as the patient went to the local "in-network" providers for services. If a patient wants to go to another doctor (specialist) out of the area, he can do that. However, there would be a higher pre-set charge to see an "out of network" doctor at a different location.

In recent years, two new types of Part C plans have emerged: Private Fee For Service plans (PFFS) and Medical Savings Accounts. They are very different from each other and from the existing plan types. Both types of plans receive a certain amount of payment monthly from Medicare. The monthly premium ranges from $0 to over $1,311 in the Inland Empire. The plans which have a deductible do not have a monthly premium, and vice-versa. Before signing up with one of these plans, one must make sure that the doctors you want are willing to accept this plan's conditions. All medical care provided under Medicare would also be provided when medically necessary under this type of plan. No referrals are necessary to go to any doctor who will agree to accept the chosen PFFS plan. The doctor and the plan do the billing to the sponsoring company, much like an HMO, rather than Medicare's method. With these plans, you appear to have great flexibility and choice of doctors. There may be some uncertainty because not all doctors and hospitals will accept this type of plan. Check to make sure!

Medical Savings Accounts are very different from any other plans. At the start of the year, the plan gives you a certain amount of money, which is put into a special (medical) savings account. The yearly out-of-pocket maximum is established and you are "locked in" to this plan for a year (or more, if you want to be). As you need medical care, you are responsible to pay for it completely out of your pocket or out of the savings account, up to the pre-set maximum amount. When that is reached, the plan will cover all further medical expenses that calendar year. If you have money left over in the savings plan, you may keep it and quit the plan. Or, you can carry it over to the next year's expenses if you decide to stay in. You will receive an additional amount for the next year. So, if you are healthy and don't use the plan's money, you'll be ahead. But, if you need medical care that's expensive, you'll have to pay up to $4,000 for it. This plan is, in a sense, a limited gamble; but you do have freedom of choice for your medical providers and where they are located.

These plans are all related to Original Medicare in what health care procedures they cover. They differ in the methods and amounts of payment and in how much freedom you have to choose your doctors and specialists. If you decide on any Medicare Advantage plan, be sure you have checked with all providers before you sign up for the year. No one wants surprises in their health care arrangements!

Medicare Part D Plans – Who Needs Them?

Medicare Part D, initiated in 2006, brought prescription drug coverage to all beneficiaries, many of whom had not had it before. Everyone in Medicare who did not have another source of continuing comparable drug coverage (like VA benefits, Tri-Care for Life, a union or employer retirement plan), was offered the choice of a myriad of private plans from drug and insurance companies. Some were available nationally, some only in one state, but the goal was that everyone in Medicare should be able to choose a drug plan they felt suited them best, unless they already had one that was comparable.

For people who choose HMO's, things are fairly simple because many managed care plans include drug plans and the contracted doctors know which drugs are listed. HMOs are not found everywhere, especially in remote areas of all states, even though there may be other types of managed care plans. Access to medications and doctors in some areas can be difficult, but all eligible people have to be offered more than one Part D plan. Of course, not all Medicare beneficiaries take drugs routinely. Those healthy folks have to make choices, too, and pay the monthly premiums. Their choice is usually very simple: They choose the least expensive plan available. In some states, people who are eligible for both Medicaid and Medicare previously had coverage for drugs, mostly at no cost (California was one such state). They, too, now have to pay for their prescriptions. The cost is low, but it can be a burden on elderly low-income people who use multiple drugs daily.

The rules for the drug benefit specify that if you don't join a drug plan when you are first eligible, you will be penalized 1% of the average national premium for every month you could have had a plan, but didn't. Those who are on both Medicare and Medicaid are assigned arbitrarily to a low-cost drug plan. Either those individuals or someone else must check to be sure the plan covers all prescribed drugs. Each plan has a different list of covered drugs (called a formulary), so the search may be lengthy.

HICAP counselors, however, have current information and can help you make your choice. Call for an appointment. There also are very helpful tools on the web. Go to www.medicare.gov and click on Medicare Plan Finder.

Other Resources

After you have read this far, I am sure you realize that helping and advising someone who needs to make a choice is very difficult. Each individual who needs or wants to choose a plan has their own ideas about what is important to them. If your family member is able to talk about what they value in a health insurance plan, you are in luck! If you already know what kind of insurance they want, or if they have communicated to you what they are unhappy about, or if they seem completely satisfied with their current arrangements, you can use the information found in the current copy of "Medicare & You" or, to make it easier, you can call your local HICAP office and make an appointment to talk to a state-registered counselor. Call 800.434.0222 anywhere in California to reach your local HICAP. Their counselors will be glad to discuss the plans and the differences among them with you. There is no cost for any HICAP service.

Our free services are available in all counties in California. Simply call 800.434.0222. Look on the Medicare website for the SHIP in your state (if you aren't in California) or call 1.800.MEDICARE. Our programs can answer your questions. They can help you understand what's important when you help others make decisions about Medicare. They can help if a procedure is denied or there is trouble with a bill. You need to talk to your *state* program because choices and rules differ.

Call 2-1-1 for information and guidance on what local organizations exist and what they cover.

---

www.cahealthadvocates.org has updated, fairly simple information on a variety of senior health insurance topics, including billing and claims, low income help, and long-term care.

Area Agencies on Aging –– Note different local names in each county (e.g. in Riverside County it is Office on Aging, San Bernardino calls it Department of Aging and Adult Services or DAAS). The statewide information number is 800.510.2020.

Social Security – benefits, eligibility (also about Medicare) – 800.772.1213. Call until 7 pm.

Legal Services – These don't cover criminal law, only civil concerns. In the Inland Empire, this agency is called Inland Counties Legal Services. Phone 888.245.4257 or 888.455.4257.

Medicare – 800.633.4227 or www.medicare.gov. (The website is usually faster and more accurate.)

Medi-Cal (or Medicaid in other states) – Call your local County Welfare Department for information. In Riverside – Dept. of Health Services – 951.955.6400. San Bernardino – DAAS 909.891.3900.

Federal Retirees' Benefits – 888.767.6738

VA Benefits and Facilities – 800.827.1000

TRICARE FOR LIFE (retired military families) 800.874.9378

Nursing Home Questions and Problems – Ombudsman Hotline 800.231.4024

Legal Issues in Nursing Homes – California Advocates for Nursing Home Reform (CANHR) 800.474.1116

Adult Fraud and Abuse – County Adult Protective Services – Consult your phone book under county government services.

Healthcare Fraud – In California, 800.434.0222 or www. smpresource.org

ARE YOU APPROACHING 65?

ARE YOU HELPING SOMEONE WHO IS ON
MEDICARE OR IS ABOUT TO BE?

DO YOU WANT TO KNOW MORE ABOUT
WHAT MEDICARE OFFERS?

YOU NEED TO CALL HICAP!

The Health Insurance Counseling and
Advocacy Program is here to help you!

We are part of Council on Aging, Southern California,
a private non-profit corporation, and we
don't charge for any of our services.

We offer free, unbiased counseling at many
senior and community centers in Riverside, San
Bernardino, and Inyo-Mono Counties.

We can help you learn how to make good choices
among the many health and drug plans.

We can help you appeal denials of care.

Toll Free: 1.800.434.0222
Local: 909.256.8369 and 760.267.1191

If you would like to become a registered Medicare expert,
otherwise known as a volunteer HICAP
counselor, call 1.800.434.0222 for details.

Notes

Medicare ID

_____

_____

Medicare Support Resources & Numbers

_____

_____

_____

_____

_____

_____

Secondary Insurance _____

Secondary Insurance ID _____

Secondary Insurance Resources & Numbers

_____

_____

_____

_____

_____

_____

Notes

6

Keeping Them at Home with Home Health Care

❧

COMFORT KEEPERS

A s the senior population grows, so does the need for support services. For many seniors, that support comes in the form of in-home care. According to AARP, 87% of adults age 65+ want to stay in their current home and community as they age.

Living at home offers seniors the ability to stay independent, but living there alone can pose certain risks, from falls and missed medications to accidents. It's a dilemma faced by many families: balancing respect for a loved one's independence with the fear that the worst could happen.

In-home care can be beneficial to seniors of any age, physical need, or acuity level. Having the assistance of a caregiver, and a customized care plan, can help seniors remain in their home and continue to experience the lifestyle and activities they enjoy while decreasing the risk of injuries or accidents.

Aging in place has other benefits as well, not the least of which is cost savings. For those who already own their homes, growing old is often much less of a financial burden. Residence in an assisted living facility can cost hundreds of dollars per day. With the help of a caregiver or private duty nurse, care dollars stretch much further.

How Can In-Home Care Improve a Senior's Quality of Life?

There's a perception that getting help with daily activities means giving up freedom, but the opposite is true. In-home care allows seniors to stay independent, live in their own home, and even improve their quality of life.

It's important to remember that seniors want the same thing we all want out of life– connection, purpose, hope, and joy. An in-home caregiver can facilitate activities, help seniors maintain social ties, and provide necessary companionship and assistance.

- Studies show that positive mental health contributes to a senior's physical well-being. In other words, enjoying life helps us stay healthy as we get older. Seniors that feel younger than their age show less brain aging, better memory, and less depression.

- Maintaining social connections should be a top priority for seniors and their families. Socially isolated seniors have a much greater risk of mental and physical decline. In fact, social isolation is as bad for someone's health as smoking fifteen cigarettes a day. In contrast, regular social interaction can have the opposite effect. Socialization has even been shown to help slow the decline of Alzheimer's disease.

- Finding ways to avoid depression and social isolation is also critical for seniors. Some of the challenges of aging can make finding joy in life more difficult; but depression has been shown to affect seniors' ability to stay engaged and active, and can make other health conditions worse. It's also associated with an increased risk of cardiac disease, fall risk, and prolonged illness.

A person's well-being depends on many factors. People are happier and healthier when they are active, connected, and feel they contribute to the world around them. When choosing an in-home care provider, it is important to know that care is customized to the individual senior, focusing on the "whole person," in order to maintain activity and engagement in life.

The engagement of the "whole person" is the philosophy behind Interactive Caregiving™–the unique manner in which Comfort Keepers® embraces the act of caregiving. The goal is to help the seniors by interacting with them in ways designed to enhance the overall health and well-being in their lives–socially, physically, and mentally.

Interactive Caregiving helps make seniors happier and healthier by making them feel needed, loved, and valued. Inspiring these feelings in the elderly cultivates a brighter outlook on life that is vital to sustaining a sense of purpose and encouraging independence.

Is it Time for In-Home Care?

The first step in determining if your loved one needs extra help is answering the right questions. Below is a list of questions to consider. Remember that there are many positive aspects to getting assistance at home, so don't be afraid to evaluate each question thoroughly. If the answer to even just one of the questions is 'yes,' it may be time to consider in-home care.

- Has there been a recent crisis?
- Does your loved one bathe less often?
- Are pills left over, or running out too soon?
- Is he/she becoming more forgetful?
- Have there been recent falls?
- Has there been recent weight gain or loss?
- Does your loved one need help walking?
- Is he/she able to run errands alone?
- Is routine housecleaning not being done?
- Have social activities diminished?

If you're considering having a conversation with a senior loved one:

- Begin early when their health allows them to fully share their wants, needs, and preferences.

- Choose a time and place that makes everyone comfortable. Avoid special family occasions or events with time constraints so that you can have a relaxed, unhurried conversation.

- Make the experience non-threatening by sharing concerns and making it clear that you want to help. Their well-being should be the focus.

- Offer options, not advice. Pose questions, listen, and offer more than one acceptable solution.

Types of In-Home Care

Depending on a client's level of need, there are different care options that seniors and their families can consider.

Companionship Care–Companionship care typically refers to non-medical in-home care with a focus on both companionship and additional services like transportation to community events or appointments, support for physician-prescribed exercise and diet regimens, fall prevention, medication reminders, light housekeeping, and grocery shopping. Companionship care is a good solution for seniors that need a little extra help around the house.

Personal Care–Personal care includes everything described under companionship care, with additional assistance for daily activities like bathing and hygiene, grooming, mobility assistance, and incontinence care.

Specialized Care–Specialized care covers a variety of needs: 24-hour care, private duty nursing, post-op care or assistance with transition home from a hospital stay, respite care, Alzheimer's and dementia care, and custom care plans built around a specific condition like arthritis, diabetes, etc.

In-Home Care Plans

One of the first questions that families ask is: What does in-home care look like for our loved one? Choosing to find care for a loved one doesn't have to be negative, but it's important to find the right provider for your needs.

In-home care providers will typically develop an in-home care plan that describes the type of care that a senior needs and documents the responsibilities of the caregiver.

Individualized care plans can increase independence and quality of life for seniors while supporting the goal of remaining in the home. A good care plan will include physical needs and non-physical health and well-being goals.

As part of the process of developing a care plan, care providers should consider the compatibility of seniors and their caregivers, and care plans should include the information that caregivers need to enrich the lives of their clients whenever possible. At Comfort Keepers®, we've had caregivers learn how to cook a client's favorite foods, help decorate for Christmas, and even plan outings to the local shelter for seniors that love dogs.

Another important piece of the care plan is family support. The plan can include activities that are built to relieve stress on a family, foster connection, and give families peace of mind. This can take the form of scheduled video chats or phone calls, transportation to visits with family, and regular updates and check-ins.

Technology is a great way to further enhance an in-home care plan. According to the US Census Bureau, in 2016, around 80% of people 65 and over lived in a household that had a computer and over 75% lived in a household with access to the internet. For seniors that like to use technology, care plans should include digital tasks and activities. For clients that are less inclined, caregivers can still use technology to play music, share family photos, and even livestream sporting events and concerts.

How Can In-Home Care Help Family Caregivers?

Many family members are taking on the role of caregiver for their senior loved ones. As society takes steps to care for our elderly population, it's critical that we also consider the needs and health of family caregivers.

A study led by the Stanford Center on Longevity and Stanford University Psychology Department, which was conducted with assistance from Comfort Keepers and Clear Care, found that for older family caregivers:

- Caring for a loved one with a mild illness generally leaves them in the same emotional state as their peers– with emotional well-being generally greater than that of younger adults.

- When responsible for a loved one with a severe illness, their reported emotional well-being tended to be lower than those of their peers.

- The cause of a decrease in emotional well-being is attributed to caregiver's inability to pursue their social goals and friendships.

The purpose of this study was to help identify the unique challenges and stressors that family caregivers face. As a partner in this research study, we reached out to the family members and decision-makers of approximately 2,000 Comfort Keepers clients.

These results suggest that older people have higher emotional well-being than younger people but not when they have a relative with a severe illness. Not all older people with ailing relatives have low well-being; rather, it depends on the severity of the relative's ailment.

Family caregivers are at risk of being overwhelmed by the responsibilities they face. As their ranks grow, it's critical that we understand their position and find solutions that can help them look after their own emotional well-being.

Caring for a family member presents a unique responsibility because of the emotional involvement of both parties. For some, enlisting the help of an in-home care company to provide respite care, or temporary care intended to relieve a family caregiver, can help family caregivers recharge so they can continue providing the type of care for their loved one that enriches the lives of both the senior and their family.

Is In-Home Care Right For Your Family?
In-home care for seniors and other adults is gaining momentum as a preferred care option. Care solutions that help seniors remain in their homes can allow aging loved ones to maintain independence, feel better, and enjoy their time in the home environment they love.

Today there are more care options available than ever before, and every provider is different. Have open conversations with your senior loved ones, find solutions that work for your family, and don't hesitate to reach out to your local in-home care provider if you have questions.

20 Questions to Ask Potential Care Providers
Ask these questions when you research an in-home care agency.

1. Do you provide care that is geared toward physical as well as mental and emotional well-being?

2. How many years have you been in business?

3. Do you keep the family informed and engaged in care?

4. Do you have a method to match a caregiver to my needs?

5. Does your agency have liability coverage? Are caregivers bonded and insured for theft?

6. Do your employees go through national and local background and driving checks?

7. Are all of your caregivers employees of your company (not contract workers), and are they covered by workers' compensation?

8. Do you have a system for tracking when caregivers arrive and leave a client's home?

9. Does your agency have a physical location where I can meet your staff, and is there 24/7 phone service?

10. Are other caregivers available to step in if our regular caregiver can't come to work?

11. Do you require a minimum number of hours per visit? If so, what is that minimum?

12. Do you offer personal care services such as dressing, bathing, incontinence care, and transfer and walking assistance?

13. Are your caregivers allowed to drive clients to appointments and social events?

14. Do you develop a customized plan of care that is updated periodically?

15. Will supervisors periodically come to our home to make sure your services are high-quality?

16. Can you give me documentation about client rights, your code of ethics, workers' compensation, HIPAA compliance, as well as your fees?

17. Do you use technology that is geared toward staying engaged and connected and ensuring safety?

18. Will you provide a home safety assessment?

19. Do your caregivers have ongoing training?

20. How quickly can we start receiving care?

He's always been the independent type. We aim to keep him that way.

At Comfort Keepers®, we provide in-home care that helps seniors and other adults live happy, independent lives in the comfort of their own homes.

Comfort Keepers.
Elevating the Human Spirit®

In-Home Care Services

- Personal and Companionship care
- Respite care
- Safety solutions
- Dementia and Alzheimer's care
- Custom Care Plans Designed to Engage Seniors Physically, Mentally and Emotionally

(800) 387-2415

Uplifting In-Home Care | ComfortKeepers.com

Notes

7

Skilled Home Healthcare

 C3

AccentCare® Home Health

Home health care delivers in-home clinical care services for those recovering from an illness or surgery, or managing a chronic condition. Skilled home health services focus on helping patients achieve their optimal levels of health and independence wherever they call home.

What is Home Health?

Home Health generally includes skilled nursing, rehabilitative therapies, and medical social work. The patient's needs and doctor-approved care plan will determine the particular services received.

Skilled Nursing

- Assessment and Observation
- Health Procedures
- Teaching and Training
- Management and Evaluation

Rehabilitative Therapies

- Physical Therapy
  Physical therapists (PTs) and physical therapy assistants (PTAs) are "body movement experts" who deliver hands-on care with prescribed exercises as well as patient education.

- Occupational Therapy
  Occupational therapists (OTs) and certified occupational therapy assistants (COTAs) deliver therapeutic interventions to help patients resume everyday activities by regaining skills that may have been affected by illness or injury.

- Speech-language Pathology
  Speech-language pathologists (SLPs) help to diagnose and treat speech, language (understanding others), social

communication, cognitive-communication (organizing thoughts), and swallowing disorders.

Medical Social Work

- Identifying Community Resources
  Identifying community resources is very helpful to patients and families who need external support. These resources help address issues such as meal delivery, living arrangements, or financial challenges.

- Counseling
  Counseling helps patients and families navigate the healthcare system, which can often seem complicated and overwhelming.

Who is Eligible for Home Health?

To be eligible for home health services, one must be:

- Under the care of a physician

- In need of intermittent skilled healthcare

- Homebound
  "Homebound" does not mean bed-ridden. It simply means that one cannot leave home without considerable and taxing effort.

Talk to Your Doctor

If you believe you or a loved one may benefit from skilled home health care, speaking to your doctor is a good place to start. Here are some good questions to begin the conversation and to discover if home health care is right for you.

- Can home healthcare help me better manage my illness?

- I take many different medications throughout the day. Can home healthcare help me better manage my medication schedule?

- I am having difficulty following the instructions for my treatment. Could a home healthcare company help me with these needs?

Considerations in Choosing a Home Health Agency

There are a number of ways you can learn about home health agencies in your area. Below are some questions you may want to ask and some resources that may be helpful.

Things You May Want to Know

- How long has the agency been in business?

- Is the agency Medicare-certified?

- What is the agency's quality star rating with CMS?

- How does the agency communicate with doctors, patients, and families?

- If applicable, does the agency have proprietary programs to address specific illnesses and conditions such as CHF (congestive heart failure), COPD (chronic obstructive pulmonary disease), diabetes, or joint replacement?

- If applicable, does the agency have special programs to address behavioral health such as late life depression or palliative care for symptom management?

Sources of Information

- Centers for Medicare & Medicaid Services
  The Centers for Medicare & Medicaid Services (CMS) created a five-star quality rating system to help those considering home health to compare agencies more easily

and identify topics about which they may want to ask questions. Visit medicare.gov/homehealthcompare to find ratings for agencies serving your city or zip code.

- Visit home health agency websites to learn more about their years of experience, services, and philosophies.

- Call home health agencies and ask for the director or manager of the office to answer questions you may have.

- Ask professionals, friends, and family for their knowledge of, or past experiences with, home health agencies.

What Happens Next?

Typically, a physician's office or a hospital discharge planner will provide you with a list of agencies that serve your area. Once your doctor has ordered home health, and you have selected the agency of your choice, the home health agency will contact you (the patient or that patient's designee) to make all of the arrangements. A Registered Nurse should call within 48 hours to set up the initial visit to assess the patient's needs, reconcile medications, and let you know what to expect.

Visits from nurses, and therapists if ordered, will be scheduled in accordance with doctor's instructions and a Case Manager will be responsible for the overall care plan. If visit schedules need to be altered to better suit the patient's needs, the agency should try to accommodate that in order to work around other appointments or commitments the patient may have.

The care plan should be customized for each individual patient. The number of home visits, as well as their frequency and type, will be tailored to the patients' needs as directed by a doctor. The length of a visit can vary depending on the services to be provided; however, generally speaking, a visit may be 45–60 minutes. Visits may include such tasks as checking vital signs, reviewing medications, or educating the patient and/or family caregivers about managing the patient's health. For those patients needing therapy, visits may include strength training, communications exercises, or teaching means for becoming more independent.

The agency should report any changes in condition to the patient's physician for consideration in modifying the plan of care. Every agency should give you a phone number for contact 24-hours a day in the event of emergent concerns. If the concern cannot be resolved by phone, you may be directed to call 911.

Should you have an unplanned emergency room visit or unplanned hospitalization, remember to contact your home health agency. This will help to keep your care team informed and will enable the home health agency to notify your physician.

Who Pays for Home Health Care

Home health care can be paid by Medicare, Medi-Cal, employer group health plans, government-funded programs, private insurance, workers' compensation, or out of pocket.

If the patient is covered by Medicare, Medi-Cal, or other third-party payers, the home health agency bills them directly, so the patient is not inconvenienced. Medicare or Medi-Cal should cover the majority of home health costs for qualified patients, including the following:

- Skilled nursing care
- Home health aide services
  Home health aide services include assistance with personal care such as bathing, dressing, and toileting.

- Rehabilitative therapy
- Medical social services
- Medical supplies
  Medical supplies might include items related to treatment such as wound dressings.

Healthcare at Home and Technology

Home health care has become a very important part of the overall healthcare system, and advances in technology support the growing demand for senior care at home.

Capabilities, such as electronic medical record access among approved parties, enhance the ability of home health agencies to communicate more easily with physicians in near real-time. This enables more expedient changes in orders, such as medication changes, if warranted.

Tele-monitoring programs enable effective care for complex patients (those with volatile or multiple conditions). With tele-monitoring, a home health agency can remotely monitor vital signs such as blood pressure, heart rate, and blood glucose level.

The goals of home health should be to deliver compassionate and quality care that results in positive patient outcomes as well as patient satisfaction, while avoiding unnecessary re-hospitalizations and emergency room visits.

The majority of seniors prefer to receive care at home over facility-based care. Fortunately, capabilities and advancements continue to make home a safe and viable setting for healthcare.

Notes

_____

_____

_____

_____

_____

_____

_____

_____

_____

_____

_____

_____

_____

_____

_____

_____

_____

_____

Notes

8

Rehabilitation

 C3

PATRICIA MEINHARDT
Ballard Rehab

When faced with a serious illness or injury, finding the most appropriate level of care can be complex and confusing, especially when you are overwhelmed with all of the feelings that emerge when a loved one is in crisis and you are responsible for helping them find the best care. Your options are to take your loved one home and be the primary caregiver for all of their needs, or find a good skilled nursing facility or acute rehabilitation care.

But how do you know which level of care is best for your loved one? Knowledge is power and knowing the difference can be critical in achieving the functional outcomes you desire—to return to the highest level of function possible.

Skilled Nursing Facilities
Oftentimes, skilled nursing facilities are providing rehabilitation services and appear to be what is recommended for care, as they do provide rehabilitation therapies and skilled nursing care.

If your loved one were recovering from a stroke and went to a skilled nursing facility, they would likely receive rehabilitation therapies for approximately 45 minutes per day for all disciplines (Occupational, Physical and Speech Therapies).

Skilled nursing facilities also require one registered nurse on duty for 24 hours for facilities with 99 beds or more. That means one nurse to care for all the residents in the facility. If there are less than 99 beds, the requirement is one registered nurse for 8 hours a day. Plus, physical and Occupational therapy can be provided for 45 minutes a day in a group setting.

The length of stay for recovery is significantly longer than that of an acute rehabilitation facility and functional outcomes are notably lower because the intensity of therapy services and level of nursing care provided are less than what someone would get with acute rehabilitation care.

Acute Inpatient Rehabilitation Hospital (IRF)

Inpatient Acute Rehabilitation (IRF) is licensed the same as major short-term acute hospital with a special designation for rehabilitation services. They offer everything with the exception of an emergency room, labor and delivery, and surgery. This designation requires the hospital to have a physician who is board certified in Physical Medicine and Rehabilitation (PM&R), called a Physiatrist, as well as a multidisciplinary team of professionals in Physical and Occupational therapy, Speech Language Pathology, Respiratory Therapy, Social Services, and even a Registered Dietician.

A Rehabilitation Hospital provides individualized care to meet the needs of patients with disabilities and other medical complex diseases. Upon admission, each patient is assigned an interdisciplinary team that develops a personalized care plan under the direction of a physician with specialized training and experience in rehabilitation. These services focus on improving the quality of the patient's life and medical conditions. Team members get to know each patient and each patient's family. In fact, family members are regarded as vital components of the treatment and healing process, so family education and counseling are a priority.

Finally, in an acute rehabilitation hospital, 24-hour nursing is provided by Registered Nurses, Licensed Vocational Nurses, and Certified Nursing Assistants under the California staffing ratio standards of one (1) Registered nurse for every five (5) patients. Nurses are also specially trained for medically complex patients, and respiratory therapists may be included.

Admission Criteria

- The patient must require active and ongoing therapeutic intervention of multiple disciplines (physical, occupational, speech therapies, or orthotics or prosthetics), one of which must be physical or occupational therapy.

- The patient must actively participate in up to three (3) hours of therapy per day at least five (5) days per week or, in well-documented cases, at least 15 hours of intensive therapy within seven consecutive day period beginning with the date of admission.

- Must require physician supervision by a rehabilitation physician.

- The patient must require an intensive and coordinated interdisciplinary approach to care.

- The patient must be motivated to participate in the program and have a discharge plan to the community.

Understanding your healthcare benefits empowers you to question post-acute options when faced with making a decision for yourself or your loved one. If you have an elective surgery scheduled and rehabilitation is anticipated, talk to your surgeon prior to surgery about the options available. Research the various levels of care and take tours of the facilities prior to surgery so you are prepared. Then, let your surgeon know your preference. If you are evaluated by an acute rehabilitation facility and approved by their medical director, but your health plan denies the admission, you may wish to contact the health plan directly to discuss your options and/or appeal the decision. They may require a physician review and, if appropriate, overturn the original decision, allowing admission.

Changes in healthcare over the years, including the adoption of the Affordable Care Act, have affected access to acute rehabilitation. Accountable Care Organizations are charged with reducing Medicare expenses and improving clinical outcomes and patient satisfaction rates. The Bundled Payment Initiative (BPI) reimburses providers with one bundled payment that must be shared among all the various levels of care, which forces providers to use less expensive levels of care. For example, over the past three years, the Centers for Medicare have designated total joint replacements as a bundle and utilize skilled nursing for rehabilitation after surgery.

Specialized Rehabilitation Programs

- Stroke (Cerebrovascular Accident CVA)
- Neurological Disorders (Multiple Sclerosis, Gilliam Barre' Syndrome)
- Dysphagia /Aphasia (Swallowing and Speech disorders)
- Spinal Cord Injury (Paraplegia, Quadriplegia)
- Spinal Surgery
- Traumatic or Non-traumatic Brain Injury
- Congestive Heart Failure
- Orthopedics
- Joint Replacement
- Fractures
- Cardiac
- Pulmonary Disease
- Medically Complex patients
- Debility related to extended illness

- Postoperative Coronary Artery Bypass Graft (CABG)
- Amputations–Post Surgical, Pre & Post prosthetic training
- Burns
- Parkinson's Disease
- Brain Injury
- Multiple Trauma
- Polyneuropathy
- Non-surgical Bariatric program up to 600 lbs.

Choosing a Provider

When choosing rehabilitation provider, it is recommended that you review their clinical outcomes. Find out what the average length of stay is for the type of illness or injury you are experiencing. Are they accredited? Check their online ratings. Don't let the big names fool you; outcomes will tell the true story. Ask for recommendations–check with friends and families to see if they have had any experience with a facility and whether they would recommend them. Ask about the patient satisfaction surveys. Inquire about specialty programs, equipment, and technology.

If you are proactive in this way, you will increase your chances of finding the best rehabilitation care for your loved one.

BALLARD
REHABILITATION HOSPITAL
A Vibra Healthcare Hospital

At Ballard Rehabilitation Hospital, we offer all these programs in a beautiful setting with care provided by clinical professionals with years of experience. A streamlined express admission process is as easy as **1-2-3:**

- **1–Call 909.473.1200** and provide the patient's name, diagnosis, address, telephone number, birthdate, social security number, insurance information, and nearest relative.

- **2–Assess.** Upon receiving the referral, our hospital will immediately:

    - provide a Clinical Liaison to evaluate your patient

    - provide after-hours and weekend assessments for all referrals

    - communicate with the physician, hospital discharge planner, and the insurance case manager to provide a prompt admission decision

- **3–Admit.** Our convenient patient-centered transition process includes:

    - working toward an efficient transfer to our hospital with a written Physician's order

    - express admission, for all medically appropriate patients, directly to our facility, without the waiting and inconvenience often accompanying Emergency Department Visits

Located at 1760 West 16th Street, San Bernardino, California, Ballard Rehabilitation Hospital has been making possibilities realities since 1972.

Notes

9

When and How to Sell the House

☎

JILL HUNTSINGER & EVA JONES
Capitis Realty

Les and Bea have three children and seven grandchildren. They want to travel more, but they worry about keeping up with the big empty house.

Ask The Tough Question:
Is it Time to Sell the Family Home?

More often than not, there comes a time to make an adjustment in an aging family member's home environment. Is your loved one ready to make a move to a more supportive environment or join the home of an adult family member who can help with their changing needs? The decision can be a difficult one, as the home often represents the place where children were raised, the safety and security of a family unit, a comfortable and familiar environment, and the physical space where the oldest and dearest memories reside. For seniors, it can signify the best years of their lives, where friends and community ties were made.

For these reasons, many may prefer to continue living in their own home or aging in place. However, some circumstances can work against this:

- Maintaining the home becomes a physical or financial burden

- A major life event makes a move the best choice

- The home becomes an unsafe environment

- An aging family member wants to be closer to family or other caretakers

- Financial concerns make it difficult to stay in the home

- Support services are not readily available

- The simple desire to have a lifestyle with more freedoms

Whatever the reason, there comes a time when a shift in life makes selling and moving on the best decision.

The most common misconception we run across is the idea that the time to call a REALTOR® is when you are ready to sell the home. The reality is that sometimes, it may take months or even years to properly prepare for this transition. Setting up trusts, handling deferred maintenance, and looking at tax implications are some of the long-term care planning conversations that can be incredibly stressful if saved for the last minute.

There's no time like the present to begin having this conversation and begin taking the proper steps.

George broke his hip, and now Norma cannot manage his needs. Their four children have very different ideas about what the future should look like.

Selling A Senior's Home is Often Different Than a Typical Transaction

Selling a senior's home can be more complicated, due to the potential of more people being involved in the process. Though seniors usually make the decision to sell, it is not uncommon for other loved ones to help them manage the process and answer these questions.

- Is moving the best alternative? If so, where? Have other options been explored?
- Are family members and close friends on board with the decision to sell?
- What is the best way to downsize personal possessions and family heirlooms?
- What are the tax-related implications of a sale?

- What effects might a sale have on future income?

The financial, logistical, and emotional considerations involved can be stressful to navigate, as the people involved in the process may feel they are in unfamiliar waters.

> *Lyle and Marie want to sell their home of forty years. Their health is declining, but the thought of moving overwhelming. What should they do first?*

What to Consider Before Starting The Process

Are all relevant parties on board with the sale and the reasons for it? It's a good idea to have a family meeting before any commitments are made. There tend to be strong emotional stakes in the sale, and a meeting may be the best thing to avoid delays during the actual process.

Have tax implications of a sale been considered? Selling a home can trigger considerable taxation. Before listing a home, you should consult a tax professional to talk over the potential implications. If you do not have a tax advisor, your real estate professional, SRES®, can provide you with a list to choose from.

Will someone be acting on behalf of the senior in the sale? In the event a senior is ill or incapacitated, a loved one will need authority to make legally binding decisions regarding the sale. A durable power of attorney must be assigned prior to the incapacity, naming a trusted one who will act on behalf of the senior.

If there are others assisting in the sale process, has one person been designated as the point of contact with professionals? It is best to have one point of contact to take the lead in communicating with your REALTOR® and other professionals. Multiple points of contact will only add confusion and potential delays in the process.

How do we begin this whole process? What are the first steps?
Find a Real Estate professional with experience in these special situations who has a network of similarly trained professional advisors. They can be invaluable at this point in time.

A Seniors Real Estate Specialist® (SRES®) will help guide you through the process and the special considerations, making the transaction less stressful and more successful.

> *Julie and Don have bought and sold homes before, but now Don is sick and can't participate. She wants a Realtor who will really support her.*

How to Find Your Seniors Real Estate Specialist® and What To Expect

First, what is an SRES®? A Seniors Real Estate Specialist® (SRES®) is a REALTOR® who is uniquely qualified to assist seniors in housing sales and purchases. The SRES® designation is awarded only to REALTORS® who have additional education on how to help seniors and their families with later-in-life real estate transactions. They also draw upon the expertise of a network of senior specialists, such as estate planners, CPA's, and elder law attorneys and are familiar with local community resources and services. Their mission is to help seniors and their families navigate the maze of financial, legal, and emotional issues that may accompany the sale of the home.

If you do not know an SRES®, it is best to ask for a referral from a trusted individual. One resource is someone that may be in a network of senior professionals such as an administrator of a senior care community, a trusted attorney, or an estate planner. If you don't have a trusted resource, simply call (800) 500-4564 or go online at sres.org to find your local Seniors Real Estate Specialist®.

Once you have identified the SRES® agent that is right for you, there are a series of common occurrences to work through as a small team. Some of your REALTOR® resource services listed in the network below will come in to play at this early stage in preparation of listing the home.

The SRES® professional network of local service providers cover a wide variety of seniors' needs:

PERSONAL: painters, landscapers, handymen, Certified Aging in Place Specialists (CAPS), clutter reduction experts, storage facilities, interior staging specialists, senior moving specialists, housekeeping services, charities, professional photographers

LEGAL and FINANCIAL: Elder law attorneys (wills, trusts, and estates), CPA's or money managers, financial planners, experts on pensions and retirement accounts, estate liquidators, tax specialists, insurance agents, 1031 exchange specialists, title and escrow companies

PERSONAL: Home health agencies, community service contracts, hospitals and clinics, public benefits offices, grief counselors, meals on wheels, PACE programs, estate sale organizers, transitional services coaches, pet boarding and dog walkers, community resources and volunteer opportunities

Ed has never owned a home. Now he has to help his parents sell their home to move into a retirement home. He's stressed and needs guidance.

Key Steps in the Process

Selling a home is rarely simple, and selling a senior's home can add some complexity. Your SRES® REALTOR® can modify some aspects of their marketing efforts to meet the individual needs of senior homeowners.

Here are the essential steps you can expect during the process:

- Listing and pricing considerations
- Staging the home
- Showing the home
- Negotiating and closing the sale

Setting a price on a home can be emotionally difficult. Some of the interpreted value of a home may be based on valued experiences there. The things one values in a home may not necessarily be in line with prospective buyers' values.

Your SRES® will offer guidance on the difficult task of finding an appropriate market price for the home. The process involves several steps: analyzing the property, comparing it to the local market, and addressing any other special circumstances surrounding the sale.

The following are some considerations your REALTOR® will use to assess a home for pricing:

FOR DATA PURPOSES: Square footage of livable space, lot size, layout, number of bedrooms/baths, location, condition, and year built.

FOR MARKETING PURPOSES: What features will attract a buyer? What makes the home stand out from the rest? Have there been any updates?

You will want to determine whether the home will be sold "as is" or Turnkey (move-in ready) or somewhere in between. Your REALTOR® will provide Active, Pending, and recently Sold comparable homes in a market analysis to help set the price in your market. The determination of the sale condition will assist in the proper pricing as well. This is a good time to have a seller's home inspection. This may uncover unknown conditions in the home due to environmental circumstances or a lack of maintenance. Both are natural to occur in every home. If there are some findings in the inspection this will give you time to either address them or make necessary adjustments to the marketing price to account for the conditions that are being sold with the home. If the home is being sold in "As Is," it should be priced appropriately if there are adverse conditions that will not be addressed by the sellers.

After documenting the home's features and characteristics, your REALTOR® will cross reference a data base of current listings and homes that have recently sold in your area. The goal is to find comparable homes that have *sold* in the last 3-6 months to determine what the marketing price will be.

It is at this time that a listing agreement and property disclosures should be executed with your real estate professional. Although the home may not be ready to go to market, you will want to have a plan to do just that and a listing agreement is a green light for you all to put the plan into motion. Remember, a listing contract can be modified if need be, as long as the parties involved agree.

Grandma Betty's craft collection is a source of great pride. Now that she needs to move in with us, what do we do with all this stuff?

Preparing for the Sale–You Only Get One Chance at a First Impression

Preparing the home for showings to the public and other realtors is called staging. The goal is to put the home's best foot forward to prospective buyers. Staging should take place before the "For Sale" sign goes up.

If you have decided to sell the home in a more "Turnkey "condition, here are some things to consider:

- Great curb appeal is a must. Regardless of your market, the home will need to draw people in. The landscape must be in good shape and a fresh coat of paint, clean windows, and colorful flowers in the beds will give a pop of wow. Your SRES® will have resources for these tasks.

- Uncluttering and Depersonalizing will only do you favors. The buyer will have a difficult time seeing themselves in the home if they are focusing on others' personal collections and family pictures. Look at it as a jumpstart on packing for the move. There are specialists in this category as well. They will help you sort, organize, pack, and move the home. They will even unpack and set up at the new location if the move calls for it. Your services are customized to the level of needs required for the seamless move of your loved one. They will often work hand in hand with estate sale companies if necessary.

- Hire a cleaning service. They will make the home sparkle from attic to basement and, in most cases, are done within a few hours. This is a huge stress reliever when you consider how much time and effort it would take to do it yourself. These people are mindful of delicate situations and will even take great care around pets if they are still in the home.

- If there are repairs needed as a result of a seller's home inspection, make them now. Your SRES® will have the referrals to capable services in the area.

Vicky has lived alone since Sid passed away, but now she can't remember to take care of her two little dogs and often forgets to eat and bathe.

Showing the Home: Open Houses and Private/Individual Tours

When a REALTOR® shows a home to a prospective buyer while the occupant is there, it tends to be awkward for both parties. For this reason, it is best to allow the home to be shown to potential buyers with just the agents present. There are often special circumstances surrounding showing appointments and your SRES® will make those instructions clear in the private area of the listing that only other licensed real estate professionals can see. For example, if you have a homeowner with special physical needs to work around, your agent will make those necessary adjustments to "appointment only" status if necessary and work within the parameters set by the senior's individual circumstances. Your SRES® works with the owner's best interests in mind and will adapt their business practices as needed.

Lyn and Ned must sell their house before they can move into a retirement home. They received an offer, but it's not what they were expecting.

The Home Has Been Successfully Marketed and Now You Have an Offer on The Table

How does a homeowner know if the offer is reasonable and serious?

First, your REALTOR® will scour the offer and verify details of the terms and financing. The next step is to review the offer with the homeowner and/or responsible parties. Your agent understands how your local market is behaving and will determine whether the offer received is one that should be seriously considered as it is written or if a counteroffer should be made, and they will help guide you through the negotiations. Remember, the negotiation process almost always requires give and take.

If there are any other parties in need of reviewing the offer, such as your attorney, they will want to look at it at this point as well.

After an offer is accepted, but well before closing, buyers will hire a home inspector to assess the condition and structure of the home. Any other inspections not done prior to listing should also be happening at this time. You will want to ensure all parties want to move forward with the purchase/sale early on in the process. Typically, this all happens within the first two weeks of your pending status. The result of the inspections may contain further points to be negotiated, such as the costs of repairs.

> *Mary's children have been by her side while she made the tough decision to sell the home and move on, but now there are more decisions about what to keep.*

Packing

Moving from the home can be overwhelming, especially if someone is facing a lifetime of possessions and making choices about what to bring and what to let go. Friends and family members can help sort through possessions, pack, and move, but sometimes a third party is extremely helpful.

Senior moving managers are a type of service provider your SRES® works with to help tend to the needs of seniors who must downsize. They will:

- Evaluate the contents of the home and assess the space in the new one
- Work with you to determine how much will fit in the new home
- Help sort and make decisions of what to keep and what to sell or donate
- Manage the process of packing and moving, then unpacking, and finally arranging the new home

Senior moving managers will help organize garage sales, arrange for donation pickups, and call for disposal services if need be. They are sensitive to the stress that can accompany this work and will often break it up in manageable steps of a few hours at a time.

For families facing the task of packing and moving on their own, think about starting the process months in advance. Set small achievable daily goals. Packing can be emotionally taxing on everyone, so consider ways to break up the work and make it more enjoyable.

Julie and Barry are excited. Everything went smoother with the sale of their home than they could have expected, and the finish line is in sight.

The "Closing Table"
The inspections are done, the buyers and lenders are ready to close, and the sellers are packed. The very end of the sale process entails:

- Buyers sign loan documents

- Funding the loan or transfer of cash
- Recording of new ownership
- Successful close of sale

Your REALTOR® will have typically negotiated for a few days after the close of the sale to deliver occupancy in order to allow time for the final move, if one has not been made yet. Within a very short time, the financial proceeds of the sale will be received. The special senior in your life is now ready to move on.

Congratulations

You have successfully navigated through the sale of the home with a very important senior in your life. We hope you have benefited from the suggestions and have found them comforting and helpful to you and your family through the process. Remember, it will be much easier with a Seniors Real Estate Specialist® at your side.

Jill Huntsinger and Eva Jones are local Realtors, with over 30 years of local Real Estate expertise. They have aligned their Real Estate practice with servicing the specific needs of maturing homeowners and their families. In order to offer their clients the most relevant and useful resources, they have earned the National Association of Realtors® designation, SRES®: Seniors Real Estate Specialist®, which affords them unique tools and market knowledge vital to servicing their clients. They are sensitive to the wide range of complex factors and unique situations associated with a life-changing move and have developed a network of vetted professionals to address virtually any scenario.

Understanding that your needs may fall outside the local service area, Jill and Eva maintain a network of dedicated SRES® certified REALTORS® who will provide their local expertise to you and your family anywhere throughout North America.

Jill and Eva are prepared to offer you and your family their diligence, professionalism, and candid advice. Call today for a confidential and complimentary assessment.

Notes

_____

_____

_____

_____

_____

_____

_____

_____

_____

_____

_____

_____

_____

_____

_____

_____

_____

Notes

10

How to Downsize and Move

ഈ

GREG GUNDERSON
Gentle Transitions

"I've been living in my home for 43 years. I've accumulated and collected things all my life. Now I'm contemplating a move to a smaller place—one-quarter the size of my current home. Where do I begin? Can I even do this?" This is the sentiment of many seniors when they are contemplating a move.

Moving is difficult for anyone of any age. Most dread the process and are pleased to have simply survived it. It ranks as one of life's most difficult events along with loss of a spouse, divorce, and job change.

For seniors, moving is dramatically more challenging. There are four identifiable obstacles to their moving process:

- leaving a home after many years
- moving to a smaller place
- diminished health
- lack of available assistance from family members

When seniors move, they are almost always leaving a home after 20, 30, or 40+ years. After so many years, moving is more than just a change in geographic location; it's an emotional experience leaving the home where children were raised, holidays took place, and precious memories were made.

During the early parts of our lives, most are moving to larger places, but during the latter part of our lives, we are almost always moving into smaller places. This brings about the most difficult aspect for seniors when making a move—making decisions about every personal possession in a home, from garden tools in the garage to china in the dining room to family photos in the den. This aspect alone is enough for many seniors to put off making a move even when they want to move for other reasons.

Most seniors face some kind of health issues as well. Even seemingly minor things like a back not working well or decreased stamina can become major hurdles to making a successful move.

Finally, in today's world, families are spread out across states and across the country or are busy with dual careers and the pace of life as we know it today. This makes assistance from family members less likely and presents yet another challenge for a senior when contemplating a move.

Taking into account the challenges noted above, it may seem that making a move for a senior is impossible. While it's not easy, it is doable. Many seniors move each year and many find they are much better off once they do. This chapter will share some of the keys to making a successful move.

Moving Tips and Techniques

Of the many challenges that arise when moving, downsizing is clearly the most difficult. Many have accumulated items of every shape and size, from photo albums in the den to collectables in the curio cabinet and papers in the office. Decisions need to be made about every personal possession in a home. Here are some tips on how to approach the decision-making process, how to select furniture for the new place, and general tips on the overall moving process.

Downsizing Tips

Take tons of pictures. It's so easy now-a-days to take pictures with a phone. Before you start a downsizing process, you or someone you know should take all kinds of pictures of your home as it exists today. This is a great solution for sentimentalists and collectors.

Believe it or not, many have said that "Having the pictures of my stuff is as good as actually having it."

Sort through easy and obvious areas first! Please don't start with the taxes and paperwork. If you do, it will take you two hours to go through two inches of paperwork and you'll feel like you could never do the entire house. Rather, start with areas that are easy and obvious. It might be things that obviously move (like from your bedroom) or items that obviously don't move (from a room that is not used). You will see success with easier areas and that will give you much-needed practice and momentum for when you tackle the more challenging areas in the home.

Be happy to sort for a few hours at a time. Even younger people find that a few hours of decision-making can be taxing. Start with small goals: "Today, I'm going to sort through the linen closet," or "This week, I'm going to sort through the kids' bedroom." Like with any large project, set yourself up for small successes.

"Isolate the variable" when decision-making. Decide first whether you want or need an item. If the answer is "no," then decide later how best to dispose of that item such as to a family member, for a sale, or to a charity. Many will look at a vase and wonder, "Do I want it or not?" and at the same time wonder if the daughter might want it or how much it might get in a sale. For most, that's too many things to think about all at one time. Focus on your own needs first; then worry about the other options later.

Assess practicality and sentimentality. Consider the practicality and sentimentally of an item.

- Items that are both practical and sentimental should move.

- Items that are neither should be left for family, sale, or charity.

- The challenge will lie in items that are one and not the other. Remember that it is the sentimental items that make our home special and that bringing those items is every bit as important as the shoes we wear and the plates we use.

Use colored stickers/labels/post-it notes to identify the disposition of items. Small colored stickers easily identify items yet are unobtrusive enough to still show a house for realtors. Stickers take a lot less time than making an exhausting list on a legal pad. The stickers are helpful to others as well. Family members can see the decisions that have been made. Movers can also follow the stickers when they arrive to know which items move and which ones don't. For cabinets, shelves, and drawers, one can rearrange items based on whether they are moving or not. For instance, "The top shelf moves and the bottom shelf does not."

Always consider available space at the new place. If you have a full kitchen now and you are moving to a place with a kitchenette, you will obviously need to downsize quite a bit. On the other hand, if your new place has a kitchen, you won't have to work so hard to pare-down. This is applicable to toiletries in the bathroom, books in the den, and any other storage areas in the house. If you have a lot of available space in the new place, don't spend a lot of time downsizing when it's not needed. Remember that built-in furniture will not be making the move with you and that you will need a place to put the items stored in that furniture in your new home.

Eliminate items that are duplicates or are the wrong size. Whether its clothes, towels, or pots and pans, it will be a benefit to eliminate duplicates or multiples of the same item. You probably will only need two or three sets of towels rather than six. Bring two umbrellas rather than five. Many of us change sizes over time (some bigger, some smaller), so eliminate clothes that don't fit anymore. Party-size kitchenware likewise can be left behind.

Floor Planning

Since most will be moving to a smaller new home, that will impact the amount of furniture they bring too. The good news is that most will make good use of the furniture they have in their new place.

Measure the new place and your current furniture ahead of the move. To avoid furniture stacked in the hallway or outside at the new place on moving day, it is very important to take measurements and make some key decisions *before* the move. Making a scale drawing can be helpful in visualizing what pieces will fit and how they might be arranged. If you have access to the new place ahead of time, you might consider taking blue painters' tape there and laying out the furniture on the floor with the proper measurements.

Be open to use furniture in different ways. Many people are so used to how a piece has been used, they can't think about it in a different way. A good example is a desk. Many have a big ol' desk from the office to do paperwork and things, but obviously don't have room for it at the new place. But they do have a secretary desk in a den that has only been used as a showpiece. In this case, the secretary desk might be converted into a working desk, take up less space, and be more attractive looking.

Consider combining furniture. For most who have been in a home for many years, they will have a living room and a den/family room. The den/family room is used daily and the living room rarely. In a smaller place, these two rooms are usually combined. Consider combining some of the furniture pieces that you enjoy every day (the favorite TV or reading chair) with a piece or two from the living room to give that a room a more "dressed up" feeling for times when friends and family visit. Living room items like a curio cabinet, nice chair, or end tables can "dress up" family room furniture. It's also okay to break up sets. Think of yourself first. If you like your bedroom set, but need a smaller bed, then get a smaller bed and keep the rest of the set. Many are too concerned about breaking up a set when the difference in resale value is actually quite small.

Avoid furniture shopping. Many think that they need to buy new furniture to fit their smaller place. Furniture shopping is not easy. It's difficult to find the right style, right color, and right size. You are moving and you're To Do List is already full. First, consider all the furniture in your current home and think out-of-the-box. You might find a piece of furniture in a used room that would be perfect for the new place. Consider bringing the love seat from the den rather than the large sofa from the living room.

Other Important Moving Tips

Understand that wanting more time is not always best. Many think they need more and more time to make the move happen— to allow time to go through everything in the house. On the other hand, allowing more time to do all that also stretches out the anxiety about the pending move, and there is a point of diminishing returns. Select a time frame that pushes you a little bit yet doesn't stretch out the process so that it becomes a drag on you.

Call charities well in advance and have a back-up plan. One might think that a charity is so happy to have your donated items that they will be right over to pick them up. Such is not the case. Plan at least a week or more in advance to schedule a pick-up. Charities understandably have become "pickier" about what they will pick up and what they won't. In most cases, the driver can decide what he takes and what he doesn't. For this reason, it's good to have a back-up plan and not wait until the very last minute for the charity to arrive.

Estate sales are usually best done after moving day. An estate/house/yard sale takes a tremendous amount of work. Arrange for an estate sales group if possible to conduct a sale after you have moved. This way, there is no confusion about what you are keeping and what is for the sale. Better yet, the estate sales group will sell everything from canned food to the washer and dryer without you lifting a finger. Check with a local realtor, church, local newspaper, or Internet to find an estate sales group in your area. Estate sales groups usually keep about a third of the proceeds from the sale, leaving you two-thirds of the proceeds, which is a bargain if you consider the amount of work involved.

Self-Storage. Storage locations are readily available and can be rented in almost any size you need. Use storage as an absolute "last resort." If you have a special family item that a niece will want when she graduates college, okay. Otherwise, most people find that it costs a lot to get things into storage, storage is expensive and, once the stuff is there, it's even more difficult to sort through.

Utility Changes. A checkbook is usually a good place to begin making the list of people you need to contact regarding your move. Your checkbook has a record of the different businesses you engage. Fill out the post card at the post office to have all your mail transferred to the new address. In most cases, you will need to change your phone number. This being the case, it's a good idea to have the old and new service overlap so that on moving day, you have phone service in both places.

Home Computer. Some want to change their computer from a desktop to a laptop to save space. Please avoid this. There are so many things changing during a move, your computer is one thing that should not change. Simply finding the "on" switch on a new computer can bring about problems and frustration.

Moving Arrangements. Ask neighbors, friends, realtors, and retirement communities for moving companies they know. Then get a written estimate from a mover or movers. Ask the mover to provide you a certificate of insurance for workers compensation and liability insurance.

Moving Day. Even before the day starts, most are drained emotionally and physically from the "build-up" to the move, so help from others can be a real plus. Recruit as much help as possible on moving day from friends and family. Leave others "in charge" for at least part of the day and allow yourself time away from the move itself. At the new place, know that the sooner you can be unpacked and settled, the more you will feel "at home" in your new environment. Family and friends can help with this process and senior move managers can be invaluable to the entire process (see below).

Senior Relocation Resources

While many seniors and family members are aware of retirement communities, realtors, and moving trucks, very few are aware that there are now services available specifically to help with the moving process.

These new companies and individuals have formed an association known as The National Association of Senior Move Managers (NASMM, www.nasmm.com).

The specialty of NASMM members is to assist seniors and their families through the moving process with all aspect of the move in a hands-on fashion. They develop floor plans, sort through belongings, coordinate with family members, make utility changes, make arrangements for items not moving, conduct packing, arrange for movers, and completely unpack and resettle the new place on moving day.

Imagine moving day at the new place, with furniture in place, boxes unpacked, pictures hung, TVs and phones connected, and the bed made. This is possible with a senior move manager and can make a dramatic difference in the moving experience.

There is Light at the End of the Tunnel

Many comment after a move that they only wish they had moved earlier. Further and to their surprise, many feel "liberated" by not having the "weight" of all their things and find themselves quite pleased with their new environment. Many find themselves invigorated by their new home and look and act younger than ever before.

While moving is not easy, it is entirely 100% doable. Many want to make a move for a number of very good reasons, but wind up delaying a move because they are intimidated and overwhelmed with the moving process. Following these tips here along with the proper planning and/or engaging a senior move manager can make the process quite workable.

And you will feel great when it's over!

Notes

11

Where Should They Live?

୧୨

DARLENE MERKLER
Placement Specialist, Merkler Consulting

There comes a time when it is either not safe for Mom and Dad to live in their own home anymore, or it's just too much work. Many of the families I have worked with over the past thirty years have parents who are still living in the 3–5-bedroom home in which they raised their children thirty years prior. Usually, there is a lot of yard work and upkeep on the house; and even if Mom and Dad are still healthy, they may be considering downsizing so they don't have the burdens of upkeep and can enjoy their retirement. But where should they go? The purpose of this chapter is to help you understand the many options available for your loved one and to help you support them as they move into this next phase of their life, taking into consideration their care needs and their ability to afford the various options.

Independent Living Communities

These are typically the first choice for a person 55 years or older. They come in several forms, and sometimes they're just a regular development of single-family homes to be purchased only by people 55 or older. (Note: Only one of the people living there must be that age.) These developments usually have a clubhouse where neighbors can congregate, have parties, play games, and enjoy themselves. There may be a monthly community fee which pays for lawn upkeep and all of the other amenities your parent doesn't want to attend to themselves.

Senior Apartments

These come in various forms as well. Most of them are just regular studio, one and two bedroom, apartments for rent, available only to those 55 years and older. These communities usually have activities going on in a recreation area as well, and some may even have bus trips available. Depending on the area you live in, the rent is comparable to regular apartments. Some of these senior apartments also offer assisted living, which will be discussed later in this chapter.

Continuing Care Retirement Communities

These communities usually consist of single-family homes and apartments for those who can live independently, but they also have assisted living and nursing home care. They cover the entire continuum of care. Most of these communities are "buy-ins," which means you pay a large amount of money up front and then "you are taken care of for the rest of your life." Don't be fooled by that statement though. It doesn't always mean what you think it does. For example, let's say your parent moves into one of these communities when they're independent, but about a year later, they need to move into assisted living. They are guaranteed a spot in the assisted living portion of the community; however, they still need to pay whatever the monthly fee is in the assisted living.

In like manner, if they are living in the independent or assisted living portion of the community and have an incident that requires going to the nursing home for rehabilitation before they return to the independent or assisted living, they still must pay their regular monthly fee while they're in the hospital and nursing home. If your parent has a three-day stay in the hospital, they should be covered under Medicare at the nursing home; but if the Medicare coverage stops, they will need to pay for the independent living or assisted living apartment as well as the nursing home.

Don't get me wrong, I think these communities are the right answer for many people. In fact, I refer clients to them often, especially if one spouse is independent and one needs assisted living or nursing home care. It allows them to be close to each other. The one who needs assistance gets it, and the independent person can still enjoy the activities that are offered at these communities. All three meals are usually provided, which is included in a monthly fee that they pay, which also includes housekeeping.

Some of these continuing care retirement communities offer different plans that your parent can come into the community under. For instance, there might be a 100% or 90% refundable plan which is higher than a non-refundable plan. What that means is that if your parent decides to leave the community, you would get back 90% or 100% of what you paid to enter. These entrance fees can range anywhere from approximately $30,000 up to $500,000 or more, depending on the community. A lot of people like this concept because they don't have to make another move, and all of their healthcare needs are met at one location.

Assisted Living

This would be a choice for someone who needs help in some area of daily care. For instance, they may need their medications managed, or help in the shower, or meals prepared, or they may need all of these things done for them. Assisted living is usually a large building with apartments. The difference between assisted living and independent living is that someone makes sure that the person gets to meals, all of which are provided (snacks too) and included in the price. There is usually a flat fee for the apartment, meals, activities, transportation, and housekeeping. An additional fee may be added depending on how much care the person needs. Sometimes the facility will outline levels of care. If a person just needs medications, the care level and cost would be lower than it would for a person who needs help with all of their daily living activities.

Most of these facilities house anywhere from thirty up to several hundred residents and are licensed by a state governing body. There are certain criteria the facility must meet in order to be licensed, and then licensing checks in on a regular basis to make sure they are complying with the outlined regulations. These regulations are called Title 22 and can be found on the local state government website. In California, it is http://www.ccld.ca.gov/, and you can look up the results of the last inspection of each facility.

Some assisted living facilities have two sections, one called General Assisted Living as well as a specific Alzheimer's Unit called Alzheimer's Assisted Living. The Alzheimer's portion of the facility is usually a secured area with specialized activities and staff that have been trained to work with those suffering from Alzheimer's disease, dementia, and other forms of memory loss. There are also Alzheimer's Assisted Living facilities that offer only Alzheimer's/Dementia care. They have no general assisted living. These free-standing dementia facilities, as well as the portion of the general assisted living facilities, have a specific type of licensing that allows them to offer care for those with memory loss.

Board and Care Homes
These are another type of assisted living facilities. They are residential homes that have been licensed under the same jurisdiction as the larger assisted living facilities, but they are private homes that usually get licensed for up to six residents. They can have private and/or shared rooms, and sometimes the owner or an assisted living manager lives at the home. In other cases, there are three shifts of caregivers who come in throughout the course of a 24-hour period. This type of facility works well for someone who may be overwhelmed with a larger facility. It is very much like living in your own home, except you're sharing it with up to five other residents. Three meals and two snacks are provided just like the larger facilities, as well as housekeeping and laundry. Medications can be managed as well as help with showers, dressing, and any other needs. Some states regulate these

facilities by the same state jurisdiction as the larger facilities, and some are regulated by the local department of aging. Some board and care homes have also been licensed to handle residents with memory loss just like the larger facilities.

If a patient has a primary diagnosis of Alzheimer's or Dementia, the facility cannot accept them unless they have that specific licensing. Make sure the facility, large or small, has that licensing if that is the type of care you are looking for because you will want a the staff has the necessary training.

Most assisted living facilities and board and care homes are paid for privately and the prices can range from approximately $4,000–$10,000/month, but there are some facilities that accept whatever the person receives for Social Security as the monthly payment. There aren't too many of these facilities out there, but they are out there. Some people may have a long-term care insurance policy that covers assisted living and/or nursing home care, but each policy is different. Some cover in-home care, assisted living, and/or nursing home care.

Assisted living facilities, large and small, may also be licensed to handle Hospice Care. That means that if your loved one needs hospice care, they can stay in that facility. A Hospice organization will then come to the facility to offer comfort measures alongside the staff at the facility. (Hospice Care can be offered in the person's home, independent living, and skilled nursing as well.) That is an important question to ask, especially if the person has memory loss. It would be very hard for them to have to move to another facility at the end of their life.

Skilled Nursing Care

A nursing home can be used for short-term rehabilitation or long-term custodial care depending on the situation. If your parent were to have an incident, they would need short-term care or rehabilitation in a skilled nursing facility. If a person needs ongoing skilled nursing care, they may need to stay in the nursing home. That would be what is called custodial care. This would be someone who does not qualify for independent or assisted living. In other words, they are bed-ridden or they need some type of skilled care such as IVs or shots daily. The cost of the nursing home can be paid for by Medi-Care, Medi-Cal, or private pay (cash) depending on the situation. See the Medicare and Medi-Cal chapters for more information. Nursing homes can cost $7500–$8333 and more per month if paying privately.

After you and your parent have decided what type of facility would be best for them, make sure that you visit at least two before making a choice. Make an appointment with the facility, take your parent(s) with you, and perhaps have lunch there. Then, visit a second time unannounced.

Below are some questions you should ask when visiting:

- How long has the company been in business? Is it privately owned or a chain? *There are advantages to both. A privately-owned business is more flexible than a chain.*

- What is the staff-to-resident ratio? *You want to make sure that the staff is not overwhelmed and can provide your parent with the attention and care they will need.*

- Is there an RN or LVN in the building or on call at all times? *Most facilities to have at least an LVN, but this is vital to the medical needs of your loved one as well in case of emergencies.*

- What types of activities are offered? Ask for a calendar showing activities. *Activities are a very important part of healthy aging. Especially in some board and care homes, residents just sit and watch TV all day. They can do that at home.*

- Ask for a menu showing meals for the month. Do they accommodate special diets? *This is part of the Assisted Living Regulations. Food is an important part of the day for older people, so make sure the facility is able to serve food your loved one will enjoy.*

- What type of training does the staff get? What is the staff turnover? *Especially in dementia care, this is key. If the staff does not get ongoing training, they may not be able to deal with certain behaviors. If most of the staff has not been there long-term, that's not a good sign.*

- Is there transportation? If so, is there an extra charge for it? Is there a charge for taking residents to doctor appointments? What outings are provided? *Not all facilities provide transportation. Some do but charge extra for it.*

- Is there a hairdresser in the building? What are the fees? *Some facilities have hairdressers, but there is almost always an additional fee for this service.*

- How are the monthly fees charged? Is it month-to-month rental? *Most facilities charge monthly with a 30-day notice policy. Most Continuing Care Retirement Communities have a large buy-in fee plus a monthly fee.*

- How much notice do I have to give if my parent wants to leave? *It is usually 30 days and it should be in the contract, but have that clarified.*

- Under what circumstances would you ask my loved one to leave? *This should also be in the contract, but ask questions about this. If your loved one declines, at what point would this facility no longer be able to care for them? If there are behavioral problems, how would they handle it?*

- How often are rates increased? When was the last rate increase? *Most facilities raise their rates annually. This can also be a negotiating factor for you.*

- Can you take your loved one out of the building? If so, what are the procedures and for how long can they leave? *You should be able to take your loved one out of the building for shopping, meals, or even an overnight stay; but facilities may vary on this policy, so make sure you ask this question.*

Notes

_____

_____

_____

_____

_____

_____

_____

_____

_____

_____

_____

_____

_____

_____

_____

_____

Notes

12

Hospice is Not a Bad Word

ℭℨ

PATRICIA MEINHARDT
VNA Hospice and Palliative Care
of Southern California

Every year millions of Americans decline hospice benefits due to lack of knowledge and understanding, which creates fear. The goal of this chapter is to empower the reader to understand hospice care benefits and alleviate this fear.

The Heart of Hospice
Hospice recognizes dying as part of the normal process of living and focuses on maintaining the quality of life remaining. It affirms life and neither hastens nor postpones death. Hospice exists in the hope and belief that, through appropriate care and the promotion of a caring community sensitive to their needs, patients and their families may be free to attain a degree of mental and spiritual preparation for death that is satisfactory for them.

When Is It Time?
The decision is often difficult for adult children when it comes to electing hospice for a loved one. It may even come as a shock when hospice is suggested for them, but if you've noticed any of the following changes in your loved one or friend, it may be time to call hospice:

- Falling
- Losing weight
- In and out of the hospital but not improving
- Sleeping more
- Having difficulty taking medications
- Has an elderly caregiver who is struggling
- Is no longer seeking curative treatment

Eligibility & Coverage
Hospice is provided by an interdisciplinary team composed of individuals who provide, coordinate, and supervise the care and

services offered by the Hospice agency. They are responsible for the periodic review and update of the plan of care for each patient. The members include the hospice physician, nurse case manager, social workers, volunteers, chaplain, home health aides, and the patient.

Individuals who meet the following criteria are eligible for admission to a Hospice Program:

1. The individual's attending physician must approve of Hospice care and certify there is a life expectancy of six months or less based on the normal disease process. Often individuals are on hospice for much longer than 6 months as they continue to show a steady decline.

2. The goal of treatment must be palliative care–to control symptoms and promote comfort.

3. The individual is encouraged to have a primary caregiver who will provide or supervise care when needed, including giving medications. If a caregiver is not available, the individual is encouraged to identify a plan for the provision of care when he or she is no longer able to perform this particular role.

Hospice is covered 100% by Medicare, Medi-cal, and most private insurances. It covers all medications related to the terminal diagnosis, medical equipment, and supplies which are delivered right to the home.

Ensuring Excellent Care

Making the right medical decisions for yourself or a loved one is crucial when you're diagnosed with a life-limiting illness. Know that you have a choice, and it is important to have the opportunity to exercise this right. Your physician should give you a list of hospice providers to choose from so that you can make this decision.

When selecting a hospice provider, ask the following questions to ensure outstanding care for your loved one:

1. Is the hospice program Medicare-certified? *Medicare-certified programs have to meet at least minimum requirements for patient care and management.*

2. Is the program licensed by the state, if required by your state? *You can check the status of licensure on the Department of Health Services website. (www.dhs.ca.gov).*

3. Does the agency have written statements outlining services, eligibility, rules, costs and payment procedures, employee job descriptions, and malpractice and liability insurance? *Ask them to send you any brochures or other available information about their services.*

4. How many years has the agency been serving your community? *Can the agency give you references from professionals such as community social workers (or a hospital) who have used their services? Ask for names and telephone numbers. A good agency will have these when you ask.*

5. How well does hospice work with each patient and family to apply policies or negotiate differences? *If the hospice imposes conditions that do not feel comfortable, it may be a sign that it is not a good fit for you. If you are not sure whether you or your loved one qualifies for hospice or whether you even want it, is the agency willing to meet with you to help you talk through these concerns?*

6. Does the agency create a plan of care for each new patient? *Is the plan of care written out and are copies given to everyone involved? Check to see if it lists specific duties,*

work hours/days, and the name and telephone number of the supervisor in charge.

7. Does the hospice provider require you to have a primary caregiver as a condition of admission? *What responsibilities are expected of the primary caregiver? Will someone need to be with you all the time? What help can the hospice offer to organize and assist the family's efforts?*

8. Does the agency explain your rights and responsibilities as a patient? *Ask to see a copy of the agency's patient's rights and responsibilities.*

9. Does a nurse, social worker, or therapist come to you to talk about and evaluate the types of services you may need? *Is this done in your home rather than over the telephone? The hospice agency should meet your needs and provide a thorough explanation of benefits.*

10. Are there references on file for home care staff? *Two or more should be required.*

11. How does the agency handle payment and billing? *Get all financial arrangements, costs, payment procedures, and billing in writing. Read the agreement carefully before signing.*

12. Does the agency have an emergency plan in place in case of a power failure or natural disaster? *Ask to see a copy of the plan.*

13. How quickly can the hospice provider start services? *The agency should be able to begin services immediately, once you make a decision about hospice care.*

14. What are the program's policies regarding inpatient care? *Which hospitals and nursing facilities contract with the hospice?*

15. Where is such care provided? *Hospice care is provided in whatever setting the patient/family call "home"–primary residence, board and care facilities, independent living facilities, skilled nursing facilities, and assisted living facilities.*

During Your First Visit

During your first visit, you should not feel rushed or intimidated to sign on to hospice. A thorough explanation should be given including what to expect, your rights and responsibilities, and a listing of team members. Be sure to ask as many questions as possible, as they should all be answered before you make your decision. The nurse completing the hospice evaluation should provide you with a complete head-to-toe examination along with a clinical history. Your assessment should be completed by a Registered Nurse. The first visit is your first impression of hospice and usually indicates the type of treatment you can expect from the hospice team.

Working with Hospice Staff

The relationship you build with the hospice staff is based on your needs. The experience should be educational, spiritual, and calming. It is their responsibility to prepare you and the patient for end-of-life ensuring comfort, care, and compassion.

Conclusion

Hospice is a benefit for all. We celebrate the birth of a child, a new life, new hope, and we can do the same at end-of-life. From the words of the "The Dash" by Linda Ellis and Mac Anderson,

"I read of a man who stood to speak at the funeral of a friend. He referred to the dates on her tombstone, from the beginning...to the end. He noted that first came the date of her birth and spoke of the

*following date with tears, but he said what mattered most of all...
was the dash between those years."*

Hospice is here to help all celebrate life, even if it is end-of-life.

Resources
VNA and Hospice of Southern California 1.800.969.4862
www.vnasocal.org

End-of-Life Care Websites
American Academy of Hospice and Palliative Medicine
www.aahpm.org

End-of-Life Palliative Education Resource Center (EPERC)
www.eperc.mcw.edu

The EPEC Project (Education in Palliative and End-of-Life Care)
www.epec.net

National Hospice & Palliative Care Organization
www.nhpco.org

National consumer engagement initiative to improve end-of-life
care www.caringinfo.org

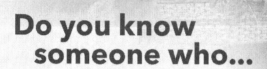

Notes

_____

_____

_____

_____

_____

_____

_____

_____

_____

_____

_____

_____

_____

_____

_____

_____

_____

_____

Notes

13

Getting Your Fears in Order: Pre-planning Funeral Arrangements

 CB

NANCY LAPOINTE

A child is born. A life begins. No two babies born share the same journey. Some are born with health challenges, some perfectly healthy. Some are born into families that have lots of other children, some are the only child. It doesn't matter what their sex, ethnic background, social status, or circumstance, each baby born is an individual. From the moment they took that first breath, their life's journey and legacy began.

How long will that journey be? Some will die young, some will live past one hundred. But the one thing we all know is that there is an end to one's life journey. There will be lots of events, challenges, joys, times of sadness, relationships, heartbreak, and new birth along the way; but in the end, whenever that is, a person will leave this world at their appointed time.

The question is: Will we be ready?

I was asked to write this chapter based on my years of experience helping families and loved ones in their advanced funeral planning. I am asking you to add this very important, end-of-life planning to your to-do list.

In 1998, I was introduced to helping families preplan their final arrangements. It became a ministry for me, as I witnessed the big difference that a little preplanning made for the families of those who passed. For the past twenty-one years, I have helped thousands of families put together their final wishes as a gift to their loved ones. I have also made my own arrangements, knowing I never want my children to find themselves sitting across from a funeral director, trying to make my final arrangements, when they have just lost their mom. I made my children's arrangements with them, knowing that I could never sit in the office and make their arrangements if I were to tragically lose one of them to an early death.

This type of planning is not easy, but it is worth it.

And the time is now, *not* when a death occurs.

I know, from personal experience, how challenging it is to be in a moment of grief and have to make these types of decisions. My brother recently died unexpectedly at the age of fifty-six, and I was challenged with making his arrangements and dealing with my siblings to try and carry out what *I thought* were my brother's wishes. Then there was my son-in-law, who lost his aunt and uncle at the ages of fifty and fifty-two when they were killed by a drunk driver. I had to meet with their three daughters to make arrangements for both of their parent's unexpected deaths because their parents never thought about preplanning. No one planned for either of these occurrences. They just happened. Unexpectedly.

When I talk to people about preplanning, these are the objections I hear most often:

- "Oh, I'm too young to think about death."
- "I don't plan on dying anytime soon."
- "My kids know what I want."
- "I have plenty of life insurance to take care of that."
- "I have money set aside so my family will not have to worry about who will pay for my funeral."
- "I am a veteran and the military will take care of everything."

In my experience, these are all excuses for not wanting to plan for something we don't want to think or talk about. And of course, it's completely understandable.

One of the hardest things I have had to deal with was the loss of both of my parents. We think our parents will be with us forever, and I was so grateful that they had preplanned when I was stunned with grief. They had put their wishes in writing, met with the local funeral home, and preplanned their arrangements. Upon their passing, the only thing the five of us children had to decide was what day we wanted to have their services.

My hope is that this chapter will inspire some conversations between you and your loved one and empower you to take the necessary steps to make sure that their wishes are carried out and you are not overwhelmed in the middle of your grief.

Why Preplan?

When a death occurs, many decisions will have to be made. Without advanced planning, the first decision will be what funeral home you want to use. If the death occurs at a hospital, the body will need to be removed within hours. If it occurs at home, the hospice person needs to know immediately who to call. If the body has been taken to the county coroner's office, when the body is ready to be released, they will want to know what funeral home to call. The last thing you will want to do in this moment is go check out several funeral homes to find the one that best meets your needs and budget. Calling and price shopping is not an option at this point. A list provided by Hospice or the hospital is just like using the yellow pages. By law, the hospital, Hospice, or coroner's office, cannot come out and recommend one funeral home over the other.

Your emotions will influence whatever decisions you make. You may be physically and emotionally drained if you have been the caretaker of your loved one. Imagine it is 2am and you are faced with these decisions. With an advanced funeral plan, you simply tell the person asking you the questions to call the mortuary, and everything will be taken care of.

Next, you will be frantically trying to come up with the money to pay for the funeral because the bank accounts are frozen and the life insurance won't fund immediately. It takes a minimum of 2 weeks for death certificates to be issued and then 4-6 weeks minimum for insurance companies to fund, which means that your family will have to pay the mortuary before the services take place.

In other words, these are the benefits your loved ones will experience through pre-planning:

1. Relieve the emotional burden of their family members. By making funeral and burial decisions in advance, they will free their loved ones from this responsibility. They will give those left behind the opportunity to spend their time grieving and supporting one another, rather than having to make decisions.

2. Express their own wishes. Often, a family agonizes over what the deceased would have wanted: "Did I do the right thing? Did I forget anything? What did my dad or mom really want to have happen?" With advanced funeral planning, a person can put all of their wishes in writing and complete all the necessary state-required paperwork to keep on file at the funeral home of their choosing. Family members are often challenged with filling in all the information necessary for the death certificate. If a person is going to take advantage of their military benefits, the funeral home needs to have on file a copy of the military person's discharge papers (DD214). Often times, one is not readily available, in which case one has to be sent for, and that takes time. A DD214 is what is faxed to the National Cemetery at the time of one's passing to get one's burial location within the cemetery secured.

3. Remove the financial responsibility from family members. Choosing a funding option is the last part of advanced funeral planning. It is a good idea to financially lock in the cost of funeral expenses, as the average funeral cost will double every ten years. By preplanning, either paying in full or using a payment plan option, one is guaranteed their costs will never go up, even though the funeral home will have price increases every year. Funeral plans are insured plans with guaranteed prices and death benefits. One can pass away while on a payment plan, and the costs of the funeral arrangements will be paid in full. Families don't have to pay the balance or continue making payments.

A funeral is important for survivors. Funerals provide an opportunity for family and friends to reflect and celebrate a loved one's life. It is the first real step in the grief process. If all the details of the funeral are planned in advance, friends and family can spend time focusing on the memories they shared with that loved one. It becomes a true celebration of that person's life.

Burial vs Cremation

The decision to bury or cremate is a very individual, personal choice. Both are just different forms of disposition. With both burial and cremation, there are so many options. More and more people are going with cremation, and I find people are trying to find the lowest cost available.

If cremation is the choice, here are a few recommendations for choosing who will handle the cremation:

- Make sure they have their own on-site crematory
- Make sure they have a local location
- Take the time to visit their location

- Meet the staff you will be dealing
  with when the death occurs

- Make sure that if, at the time of death, your
  family wants to have a private family viewing,
  the company can accommodate your wishes

It is always best to make sure all your questions are answered before you sign on with a company that is going to handle the final disposition of your loved one. It is very important to know your loved one's wishes and carry them out. It is not about you. It is about what your loved one wants. Don't let cost prevent you from honoring their wishes. Simply plan ahead.

Question to Start the Preplanning Process

When we die, we want to be remembered in our own way. That's why it is so important to *Have the Talk of a Lifetime* and let loved ones share with you exactly how they want to be remembered. Having this conversation now will significantly reduce the stress for loved ones when it comes time to make service arrangements. Be patient. Listen. Make sure they know that you want to respect their wishes. Let them tell you what they would like to have happen. Keep in mind that they are dealing with the reality of the end of their life's journey. With the right approach you can bring them peace of mind knowing they have been able to express their wishes.

Here is a list of questions to get the conversation started with your loved one:

- How do you want to be remembered?

- What would you like at your memorial service?

- How would you like your loved ones to
  celebrate your life when you die?

- Do you have a favorite charity you would like people to donate to in your honor?
- Would you like anyone in particular to speak at your memorial service?
- What would your theme song be? Is there specific music you'd like played at your service?
- Where would you like the service to be held?
- Do you want a religious or non-religious ceremony?
- Do you want to be buried or cremated?
- How do you want your cremated remains to be handled?
- Where do you want your final resting place to be?
- Do you want a headstone marker? What would you like it to say?

If your loved one has made arrangements with a funeral home already, it is best to look over that paperwork. Things change, times change, and their wishes may have changed. Now is the time to review, confirm, and make necessary changes to truly carry out their wishes. Learn what was not included in the original advanced funeral plan so you can be prepared and plan on how you are going to cover those additional costs.

Often times, people think, "I bought my cemetery property, I have a will, I have a living trust, I have life insurance;" and in their minds, everything is taken care of. As a caregiver, it is best to review all of what they have done so far.

- Living wills and trusts list an individual's financial affairs and or medical care and treatment. They are not written for the benefit of funeral planning and costs.

- Insurance policies are in place to offset the cost of living for a surviving spouse when social security and pension income stops upon the death of the loved one. If one thinks their life insurance policy is in place for funeral expenses, keep in mind that life insurance policies do not lock in the cost of funeral expenses nor do they fund immediately upon death.

- Purchased cemetery property doesn't usually include the additional costs of opening and closing the grave, endowment care, vaults, or the headstone. Confirm what your costs will be at the cemetery, so you can be prepared and plan on how you are going to cover those additional expenses.

- If you are planning a service at your church of choice, confirm their fees for the use of the church, music, and clergy support. Most churches do charge, so be prepared and plan on how you are going to cover those additional expenses.

I hope this information has helped to make advanced funeral planning a priority for you, your loved ones, and your family. Advanced planning is not just for those that are old, sick, or diagnosed terminal; we are all going to die, we just don't know when that will be. We all need to do our preplan. Planning ahead will save a lot of heartache, grief, and even family disagreements. Find someone you feel comfortable with and can trust with helping you to carry out your loved one's wishes. Seek a person with experience that can help you with your decision making. Talk to friends, family, and church members to get recommendations from their past experiences. Do your due diligence and find a funeral home that will treat you with care and compassion, like you are part of their family.

Planning ahead will make final arrangements a true celebration of the life of your loved one.

Preneed Associates of Southern California

Helping Families Preplan Funeral Arrangements in Advance

Nancy Lapointe
Advanced Planning Advocate

For the past 22 years I have been meeting with families to help them put all their wishes in writing, and to complete all the state required forms necessary at the time of one's passing. I have helped families through their decision making process whether it be for burial or cremation. With so many options to choose from my role is to make their decision making process as easy as possible. My ultimate goal is to assure a person that their wishes will be carried out by their loved ones. I educate them on the process, guide them in their decision making, and share with them that preplanning is a gift that they will be giving to their spouse, children, family and friends. I am available to meet with families in the comfort of their home, or at the funeral home whichever works best. There is no cost or obligation for an appointment.

951-285-5579
Email: nancyfuneralplans@yahoo.com
Licensed by the State of California

Notes

_____

_____

_____

_____

_____

_____

_____

_____

_____

_____

_____

_____

_____

_____

_____

_____

_____

Notes

_____

_____

_____

_____

_____

_____

_____

_____

_____

_____

_____

_____

_____

_____

_____

_____

_____

_____

_____

PART 2

❧

Resources for Caregivers

14

Department of Aging Resources

CB

THE NATIONAL OFFICE ON AGING

The Administration on Aging (AoA), an agency in the U.S. Department of Health and Human Services, is one of the nation's largest providers of home- and community-based care for older persons and their caregivers. Our mission is to develop a comprehensive, coordinated, and cost-effective system of long-term care that helps elderly individuals to maintain their dignity in their homes and communities. Our mission statement also includes helping society prepare for an aging population.

Created in 1965 with the passage of the Older Americans Act (OAA), AoA is part of a federal, state, tribal, and local partnership called the National Network on Aging. This network, serving about 7 million older persons and their caregivers, consists of 56 State Units on Aging; 655 Area Agencies on Aging; 233 Tribal and Native organizations; two organizations that serve Native Hawaiians; 29,000 service providers; and thousands of volunteers. These organizations provide assistance and services to older individuals and their families in urban, suburban, and rural areas throughout the United States.

While all older Americans may receive services, the OAA targets those older individuals who are in greatest economic and social need: the poor, the isolated, and those disadvantaged by social or health disparities.

Six Core Services Funded By the OAA

Supportive services enable communities to provide rides to medical appointments, and grocery and drug stores. Supportive services provide handyman, chore, and personal care services so that older persons can stay in their homes. These services extend to community services such as adult day care and information and assistance as well.

Nutrition services include more than a meal. Since its creation, the Older Americans Act Nutrition Program has provided nearly 6 billion meals for at-risk older persons. Each day in communities across America, senior citizens come together in senior centers or other group settings to share a meal, as well as camaraderie and friendship. Nutrition services also provide nutrition education, health screenings, and counseling at senior centers. Homebound seniors are able to remain in their homes largely because of the daily delivery of a hot meal, sometimes by a senior volunteer who is their only visitor. March 2002, marked the 30th anniversary of the OAA Nutrition Program, and AoA will be celebrating this successful community-based service throughout the year.

Preventive health services educate and enable older persons to make healthy lifestyle choices. Every year, illness and disability that result from chronic disease affects the quality of life for millions of older adults and their caregivers. Many chronic diseases can be prevented through healthy lifestyles, physical activity, appropriate diet and nutrition, smoking cessation, active and meaningful social engagement, and regular screenings. The ultimate goal of the OAA health promotion and disease prevention services is to increase the quality and years of healthy life.

The National Family Caregiver Support Program (NFCSP), funded for the first time in 2000, is a significant addition to the OAA. It was created to help the millions of people who provide the primary care for spouses, parents, older relatives and friends. The program includes information to caregivers about available services; assistance to caregivers in gaining access to services; individual counseling, organization of support groups and caregiver training to assist caregivers in making decisions and solving problems related to their caregiving roles; and supplemental services to complement care provided by caregivers.

The program also recognizes the needs of grandparents caring for grandchildren and for caregivers of those 18 and under with mental retardation or developmental difficulties and the diverse needs of Native Americans.

Services that protect the rights of vulnerable older persons are designed to empower older persons and their family members to detect and prevent elder abuse and consumer fraud as well as to enhance the physical, mental, emotional, and financial well-being of America's elderly. These services include, for example, pension counseling programs that help older Americans access their pensions and make informed insurance and health care choices; long-term care ombudsman programs that serve to investigate and resolve complaints made by or for residents of nursing, board and care, and similar adult homes. AoA supports the training of thousands of paid and volunteer long-term care ombudsmen, insurance counselors, and other professionals who assist with reporting waste, fraud, and abuse in nursing homes and other settings; and senior Medicare patrol projects, which operate in 47 states, plus the District of Columbia and Puerto Rico. AoA awards grants to state units on aging, area agencies on aging, and community organizations to train senior volunteers how to educate older Americans to take a more active role in monitoring and understanding their health care.

Services to Native Americans include nutrition and supportive services designed to meet the unique cultural and social traditions of tribal and native organizations and organizations serving Native Hawaiians. Native American elders are among the most disadvantaged groups in the country.

Eldercare Locator

Additionally, AoA supports the Eldercare Locator, a national toll-free service to help callers find services and resources in their own communities or throughout the country. That number is 1.800.677.1116.

Each town and city offer a range of supporting services available to older residents 60 years of age or over. Local Information and Assistance Programs and/or Area Agency on Aging can assist older persons and their families in locating the services they need. Some of the services available include:

Adult Day Care: Adult Day Care Centers offer social, recreational, and health-related services to individuals in a protective setting who cannot be left alone during the day because of health care and social need, confusion, or disability.

Caregiver Programs: The National Family Caregiver Support Program provides programs and services for caregivers of older adults and some limited services to grandparents raising grandchildren.

Case Management: Case managers work with family members and older adults to assess, arrange and evaluate supportive efforts of seniors and their families to remain independent.

Elder Abuse Prevention Programs: Allegations of abuse, neglect, and exploitation of senior citizens are investigated by highly-trained protective service specialists. Intervention is provided in instances of substantiated elder abuse, neglect, or exploitation.

Financial Assistance: There are benefit counseling programs that can be accessed through the (I&R/A) specialist at your local area agency on aging to assist older adults with financial assistance.

Home Health Services: Home health care includes such care activities as changing wound dressings, checking vital signs, cleaning catheters, and providing tube feedings.

Home Repair: Programs that help older people keep the condition of their housing in good repair before problems become major. Volunteers might come to an individual's home and patch a leaky roof, repair faulty plumbing, or insulate drafty walls.

Home Modification: Programs that provide adaptations and/ or renovations to the living environment intended to increase ease of use, safety, security, and independence. There are some local, state, Federal and volunteer programs that provide special grants, loans, and other assistance for home.

Information and Referral/Assistance Information Services (I&R/A): Information Specialists are available to provide assistance and linkage to available services and resources.

Legal Assistance: Legal advice and representation is available to persons aged 60 and over for certain types of legal matters including government program benefits, tenant rights, and consumer problems.

Nutrition Services: Home Delivered Meals, popularly known as "Meals on Wheels," are nutritious meals delivered to the homes of older persons who are homebound. Congregate Meals provide the opportunity for persons aged 60 and over to enjoy a meal and socialize with other seniors in the community.

Personal Care: Services to assist individuals with functional impairments with bathing, dressing, shopping, walking, housekeeping, supervision, emotional security, eating, and assistance with securing health care from appropriate sources.

Respite Care: Respite is relief or rest, for a specified period of time, from the constant/continued supervision, companionship, therapeutic, and/or personal care of a person with a functional impairment.

Senior Housing Options: The decision to seek care outside an individual's home is a difficult one. If you are considering such a move for yourself or a family member, please contact your local area agency on aging I&R/A specialist to determine the full range of support options available to you.

Senior Center Programs: Senior Centers offer a variety of recreational and educational programs, seminars, events, and activities for the active and less active older adult.

Telephone Reassurance: Provides regular contact and safety check by trained volunteers to reassure and support senior citizens and disabled persons who are homebound.

Transportation: Programs that provide door-to-door transportation for people who may be elderly or disabled, who do not have private transportation, and who are unable to utilize public transportation to meet their needs.

Volunteer Services: There are numerous volunteer programs and opportunities available for older adults such as daily telephone reassurance, friendly visiting. and insurance counseling.

There is a wealth of information on the Internet designed to assist family members and caregivers of older adults.

Alzheimer's Association CareFinder

This site assists those caring for someone who has Alzheimer's disease in finding good care in their community.

- www.alz.org/carefinder

Family Caregiver Alliance

This site contains a wide array of publications and services based on caregiver needs, including a Family Care Navigator.

- www.caregiver.org

Family Caregiving 101

This site is designed to provide caregivers with the basic tools, skills and information they need to protect their own physical and mental health while they provide high quality care for their loved one.

- www.familycaregiving101.org

National Alliance for Caregiving

This site contains publications and resources for caregivers, including the Family Care Resource Connection, where you can find reviews and ratings on over 1,000 books, videos, websites, and other materials on caregiving.

- www.caregiving.org

National Family Caregivers Association

This site offers a virtual library of information and educational materials for family caregivers.

- www.thefamilycaregiver.org/caregiving_resources

Administration on Aging

Administration on Aging
Washington, DC 20201
Phone: 202.619.0724

Office of the Assistant Secretary for Aging
202.401.4634

Public Inquiries
202.619.0724

Eldercare Locator
(find services for an older person in his or her area)
800.677.1116

AoA Fax
202.357.3555

Federal Relay Services
1.800.877.8339 (Off Site)

AoA's Regional Offices
(requests for information about aging issues and AoA programs)
E-mail: aoainfo@aoa.hhs.gov www.aoa.gov/about/about.aspx

Notes

15

VA Benefits

 са

ESTHER WANG
Elder Law Attorney

According to a study by the National Care Planning Council, at least 25% of the geriatric patients in the U.S. are either wartime veterans or widows of wartime veterans. Many of them need long-term care, yet over half of them are unaware of a VA benefit commonly known as the Aid and Attendance pension benefit. This can be awarded by the VA to a claimant to help pay for assistance at home, in an assisted living community (including memory care and board), and in a skilled nursing facility.

The VA will pay up to the **maximum** amounts indicated below on a monthly basis for a claimant who is eligible for the Aid and Attendance pension benefit:

Single Wartime Veteran	$1,881
Married Wartime Veteran	$2,230
Widows or Widower of Wartime Veteran	$1,209

(The figures above are correct as of June, 2019, and are subject to change by the VA.)

However, it has been reported that the application for the pension benefit often takes more than one year to approve; for some, the wait to receive such benefit takes more than five years. The Aid and Attendance pension (hereinafter A & A pension), intended to support or subsidize the daily care of elderly wartime veterans or their spouses, is riddled with problems, including delays and confusing paperwork.

The purpose of this chapter is to provide a brief overview of the legal requirements that must be met and the documents that need to be submitted to the VA Pension Management Center in order for a claimant, either a wartime veteran or a widow (or widower) of a wartime veteran, to qualify for the A & A pension benefit. When you follow the advice of an experienced VA accredited attorney, an application can be approved within eight months following the submission, and often much quicker.

Generally, there are four requirements that a claimant needs to meet before he or she can be eligible to receive A & A pension benefit:

1. Status as a wartime veteran or a widow or widower of a wartime veteran;

2. Permanent disability of the claimant and his/her need for care;

3. Income eligibility requirement; and

4. Net worth eligibility requirement.

Status as a Wartime Veteran or a Widow of Widower of a Wartime Veteran

In order to qualify for the A & A benefit, you must be either a wartime veteran or a widow (or widower) of a wartime veteran.

Wartime Veteran

In order to prove that you are a wartime veteran, you must have served at least 90 consecutive days in active duty, and at least one day of which is during a period of war. You must have been discharged for reason other than dishonorable.

A period of war is defined as any of the following:

1. **World War I.** April 6, 1917 through November 11, 1918, inclusive. If the veteran served with the U.S. military forces in Russia, the ending date is April 1, 1920. Service after November 11, 1918 and before July 2, 1921 is considered World War I service if the veteran served in the active military, naval, or air service after April 5, 1917 and before November 12, 1918.

2. **World War II.** December 7, 1941 through December 31, 1946, inclusive. If the veteran was in service on December 31, 1946, continuous service before July 26, 1947 is considered World War II service.

3. **Korean Conflict.** June 27, 1950 through January 31, 1955, inclusive.

4. **Vietnam era.** The period beginning on February 28, 1961, and ending on May 7, 1975, inclusive, in the case of a veteran who served in the Republic of Vietnam during that period. The period beginning on August 5, 1964 and ending on May 7, 1975, inclusive, in all other cases.

5. **Mexican border period.** May 9, 1916 through April 5, 1917, in the case of a veteran who during such period served in Mexico, on the borders thereof, or in the waters adjacent thereto.

6. **Persian Gulf War.** August 2, 1990 through date to be prescribed by Presidential proclamation or law.

Documents that you need to prove your wartime veteran status:

1. **The original copy or a certified copy of the discharge paper, or the DD 214 Form.** On the DD 214 Form, it states your date of entry into active duty and when you are discharged from active duty. The DD 214 must state that you serve at least 90 consecutive days in active day and at least one day during a period of war. The DD 214 Form also states whether you were honorable, generally or medically discharged. A person who is dishonorably discharged will not be eligible for A & A pension benefit.

2. **Identifications.** You will need to provide a copy of your identification, like driver's license or senior citizen's card issued by the DMV, social security card and Medicare card to prove your identity.

Documents that you need to prove your marital status: The VA is entitled to know all about your marital history. You will need to provide, for each marriage that you have, the marriage certificate, death certificate or the divorce judgment.

Widow (or Widower) of a Wartime Veteran

In order to prove that you are a widow (or widower) or a wartime veteran, you must prove it by providing the documents listed below:

1. The DD 214 Form of your deceased spouse showing that he or she was a wartime veteran (see the criteria for wartime veteran indicated above);

2. You and your spouse's marriage certificate;

3. Your spouse's death certificate, on which it is indicated that you are the surviving spouse.

4. Identifications: You will need to provide a copy of your driver's license or senior citizen's card, social security card, and Medicare card to prove your identity.

While there are exceptions to the rule, generally speaking, if the surviving spouse of a wartime veteran remarried, the surviving spouse would not meet the requirement as a widow or widower of a wartime veteran.

Permanent Disability of the Claimant and His or Her Need for Care

Simply put, in order for you to qualify for A & A pension benefit, you must be permanently disabled and require regular aid and attendance of another person. This can be care that you receive in your home by a paid caregiver, and the paid caregiving can be delivered by a home care agency or a family member (but not a spouse). This can also be care that you receive in an independent living community, assisted living community, or memory care community.

Medical evidence must be submitted in order to prove the need for care. The law also requires that the medical evidence be internally consistent. This usually means that your physician's reports or records and the caregiver's statement must be consistent in order for claim to be approved by the VA.

Income Eligibility Requirement

Generally speaking, to determine whether you meet income eligibility in order to qualify for pension benefit, VA counts all of your income (if you are single) and your spouse's income (if you are married) and then deducts the sum of the incomes by your recurrent caregiver expenses and recurrent medical expenses to arrive at a "countable income." An example will be helpful here.

Let's say your and your spouse's combined income is $5000, which includes social security benefit and pension. Your monthly medical deductible is $200 and you pay either a home caregiver or an assisted living community (or memory care community) $4500 to take care of you. In this hypothetical case, your countable income is $300 ($5000–$200–$4500 = $300).

The countable income is then compared with the maximum benefit amount. If the countable income is lower than the maximum benefit amount, then you will be approved for the difference between the maximum benefit amount and the countable income. If the countable income is above the maximum benefit amount, the claim will be denied.

For the example above, if you are a married wartime veteran with a countable income of $300, your benefit will be $1,930 ($2230–$300 = $1930).

To prove your eligibility, you will need to submit to the VA Pension Management Center the following:

1. Income information, such as social security statement and pension statements;

2. Caregiver or facility statement and copies of the checks made to the caregiver or facility.

3. Bank statements that show the payments to your caregiver or facility.

Net Worth Eligibility Requirement

In order to be eligible for the A & A pension, you must have a net worth below the allowable limit. The VA has set the allowable limit for net worth at $127,061 effective December 1, 2018. (The current limit will always be published on the VA's website at www.benefits.va.gov/pension/.) The VA will deny or discontinue A & A benefit if the net worth of the claimant is above the allowable limit.

If you are a single individual, then only your assets will be counted. If you are married, then the assets owned by you and your spouse will be counted.

The term "net worth" means the sum of the claimant's assets _**and**_ annual income. Assets are defined to be the fair market value of all property owned by the claimant, including all real and personal property. The fair market value of the property is reduced by any mortgages or encumbrances to each specific property.

However, your primary residence, if it sits on a lot that does not exceed two acres, will not be counted towards net worth. Likewise, one vehicle and personal effects will not be counted towards net worth.

Transfers of Assets

In the past, claimants who wish to qualify for A & A benefit that have too many assets can transfer their assets out of their names and then qualify for benefit. Under the new law which went into effect on October 17, 2018, transfers are subject to calculations of penalty, which is the equivalent of periods of ineligibility. While the applications of the new rules should be done in a case-by-case manner and every case should be carefully analyzed and planned by an experienced elder law attorney, generally speaking, if you legally transfer assets out of your name and then wait three years before applying for A & A pension benefit, the transfers would not incur a period of ineligibility. Therefore, if you have more assets than what is allowed by the net worth eligibility requirement, it would be prudent to plan ahead and legally transfer assets out of your name by an irrevocable trust, wait three years after the transfer, and then apply for the benefit.

Planning Ahead

It is important to assess whether you can qualify for the A & A benefit before you apply for it. It is preferable to plan your long-term care ahead of time. When planning ahead, you can incorporate VA A & A benefit into your overall plan to see how it can benefit you in the long run and what steps you need to take at this time to preserve assets so that they will last longer.

Finally, you and your loved one made sacrifices for our country. We thank you for your sacrifices. You have indeed earned this benefit. Let's put it to work for you when you need it the most.

Notes

16

Reverse Mortgages Aren't What You Think

CB

Don McCue
Reverse Mortgage Specialist

Is a Reverse Mortgage Right for You?

If you are married and one spouse is at least 62 years old, single, or widowed, divorced (6 months or more) and 62 years old, you may be eligible for a reverse mortgage loan approval. Reverse mortgages are a way to borrow against the equity in your home, using a current appraised value minus any mortgage debt you may now owe. Your income and credit score may be a factor since property taxes and insurance must still be paid. Independent counseling is required in advance, so please consult your advisor prior to doing this to make sure it is the best choice for you.

Potential Advantages of a Reverse Mortgage:

- It may help your financial independence and maintain or improve your quality of life.

- It allows you to remain in, and keep, control and the title to your home.

- The money you receive is generally not considered taxable income. You should consult with an independent tax professional to determine your individual tax consequences.

- You do not have to make any payment until the end of the term of the loan (defined to be when the last eligible borrower on the reverse mortgage loan permanently leaves or sells the home, or dies); or the loan ends by failure to pay property taxes and insurance on time or due to a catastrophic event. Of course, you can choose to pay on the balance whenever if you wish.

- You can eliminate existing mortgage payments by paying off current loans through proceeds from your new reverse mortgage.

- You can select from many flexible options to receive your loan proceeds to meet your needs.

- Unused dollars can stay in your Reverse Mortgage LOC (Line of Credit), earning tax-free growth to protect against future long-term care cost and other retirement needs. This is a huge benefit that means with good early planning, a reverse mortgage should not be delayed until it is the last resort!

Potential Drawbacks of a Reverse Mortgage:

- These are sometimes more complicated than a conventional mortgage, but isn't everything that way today? This is not a one-size-fits-all deal. Each individual's and family's circumstances (i.e. health, age, retirement savings and heirs) are important issues to be discussed.

- We hear they are expensive because they are typically FHA insured (a good thing) and those costs are paid upfront; however, there are "non-FHA" programs as well for some borrowers.

- Although the loan proceeds are typically income tax-free, *it may affect your eligibility under existing law for "need based" public assistance benefits such as Supplemental Security Income("SSI") and MediCal/ Medicaid.* Please consult your advisor.

- Be aware that there is "no free lunch." A reverse mortgage may reduce or even eliminate the equity in your home, *affecting the estate to be distributed to your heirs.*

- When the loan is other than an FHA- insured mortgage, you should confirm the Reverse Mortgage is *entirely a non-recourse loan.* This means the amount to be repaid is limited only to your home's current appraised value and loan amount at the time of sale, transfer of title, or death of last eligible borrower. Neither the borrower(s) or your heirs' estate's assets or income can be resources subject for repayment. It is a contract based only on the home.

We are attempting to educate and rid people of some of the myths and misconceptions that lead to reverse mortgages being misunderstood, often even by real estate, mortgage, tax, financial advisor and legal professionals. Check out their experience before accepting the advice and opinion.

Important Questions to Ask Before Choosing a Reverse Mortgage:

- How much money will I need?
- Is there a way to meet my needs and protect myself in the future that does not involve a reverse mortgage?
- Will a reverse mortgage make me or a co-borrower ineligible for any "needs based" public assistance benefits–now or in the future?
- Do I and my home qualify for a reverse mortgage? The right originator can tell you in about 10 minutes.
- How much can I expect to qualify for?
- What will my origination fees, closing cost, interest rate (monthly or periodic) cost be, and how are they paid for?
- Will I ever have to sell my house before I want to in order to pay the reverse mortgage?
- Can the lender ever take my house instead of it going to my heirs or charity of my choice?
- When I die, what happens to people still living in my home? Will they have to leave or sell the house, or can they refinance and keep the home?

- Will the reverse mortgage become due and payable if I require long-term care and move into an assisted living facility?

- Will there be anything left for me or my heirs if and when the reverse mortgage is paid off?

- Can I sell my house and pay off the reverse mortgage. Are there any pre-payment penalties?

Types of Reverse Mortgages:

- FHA-insured mortgage: *H*ome *E*quity *C*onversion *M*ortgage (HECM) fixed or variable rates.

- Non-FHA-"UNINSURED" proprietary *"jumbo"* reverse mortgages for higher-valued properties. Even the seemingly wealthy can be "property rich" and cash flow poor!

- Reverse Mortgage **PURCHASE** loan: Yes, buy your next home and upgrade (or downsize) using a reverse mortgage loan approval that goes right into escrow with your purchase offer. You own your home–the bank doesn't! It will go to your heirs with a proper Living Revocable Trust or Probate (if no estate planning has been done). Best of all, live in your dream home with NO mortgage payment for the rest of your lives!

Important Things To Do Before You Make a Decision:

- Decide how long you intend to stay in your home, why, and what could change.

- Consult a HUD approved Reverse Mortgage counselor (required). All licensed loan originators help with this by providing an approved list for your consideration.

- Understand your reasons for getting a reverse mortgage, not only from a need based consideration but a long-term care and retirement security based discussion. Using tax-free money from Reverse mortgage LOC and using less from your IRA or 401k can help your money last longer. Consult your advisor for retirement portfolio optimization strategies.

- Include trusted family members and your team of trusted advisors (i.e. attorney, CPA/accountant, financial advisor, and mortgage loan officer) in talks together.

- Understand that a reverse mortgage is NOT a good retirement plan but a supplement to it. There is no substitute for good early, ongoing, well-thought-out planning.

- Start now to be an advocate for ***planning for the best*** and ***preparing for the rest***!

Call us today and we can help you through this discussion.

- www.aarp.com
- www.canhr.org
- https://www.nrmlaonline.org
- https://www.theamericancollege.edu

Notes

17

Mental Health Challenges

೫

DR. PAUL MCMAHON

Aging, in and of itself, brings about terrific changes across every aspect of our lives. Biologically, socially, spiritually, and psychologically, we grow, we push forward, and sometimes we fall. Time hands us regular opportunities and challenges we must face; and the mental health challenges related to aging, like medical dilemmas, can often be met successfully and conquered with the right resources, support, and knowledge.

Speaking in general terms, our mental health usually doesn't change drastically. People who are happy in their youth are typically happy in their retirement. Anxious teenagers grow up to be anxious adults. Those beset by more serious emotional issues like schizophrenia or bi-polar depression in their young adulthood tend to be challenged by those imbalances their whole lives.

More typical than drastic psychological changes are the unhurried, more insidious problems that slowly grow into our personalities and create unhappiness for ourselves and those around us. A man once able to "let things slide" is now more frequently depressed. A woman who once rarely drank is now hiding her heavy alcohol use from those around her. A couple that once experienced a little tension is now overwhelmed with anxiety. Mental health issues, like heart disease or isolation, sneak up on us and take hold of our lives.

While there are dozens of serious mental health concerns that can interrupt the lives of older adults, most can be narrowed down into five larger overlapping categories: 1.) Depression, 2.) Anxiety, 3.) Psychosis, 4.) Substance abuse, and 5.) Dementia. Often, we endure only a minor inconvenience of just one of these dilemmas; but sadly, we're often faced with two or more of these issues hitting us or our loved ones at once. Early recognition of the symptoms of these mental health problems is a key to managing them wisely, and knowing what to do about each of them can be life-saving.

Depression

Perhaps the singular psychological concern most associated with growing old is unhappiness. Many wrongly consider it inevitable that we will grow bitter and grumpy the older we get. And while it's true that we certainly have more challenges as we age, and maybe more things to be depressed about, we also have more experience "rolling with the punches" and coping strategies we didn't have in our youth. However, it is true that a good portion of the elderly generation experience depression.

Symptoms of depression usually include loss of energy, isolation, feelings of sadness, changes in our daily routines, and hopelessness. More profound cases of depression can even include thoughts of suicide. Incredible unhappiness, or "Major Depression," as it's called in the field of psychology, is far rarer than the depression we might complain about to our friends and families when we've endured a loss or are simply feeling down. There is no fault in calling ourselves depressed when indeed we're rightfully feeling depressed, but that is never to be confused with the often-crippling psychological problem of Major Depression. Feelings of depression are often normal; Major Depression is not. It is a mental health problem that warrants attention and intervention from professionals trained to diagnose and treat this intense level of sorrow.

Steps to overcome depression, whether the somewhat benign feelings we experience when encountering losses, or the Major Depression that is a bona fide mental illness, are similar. If you or a loved one are depressed, the first step is recognizing that these emotions are unusual and should be faced, not denied. The second step is talking about one's feelings and symptoms to a supportive friend, confidant, or therapist. If one doesn't do anything about their symptoms, they can't expect them to change; and one of the easier ways to overcome them is to simply talk about those symptoms to somebody who cares. Often, merely putting our feelings into words has a curative effect. In addition to talking with others, activity is also a great healer. It's important for those beset with depression to get out into the sunshine, rekindle old hobbies (especially social ones), and force themselves to move a bit more. To feel alive again is crucial. If the level of unhappiness has the person feeling absolutely crippled or they're having thoughts of death, then working with a psychologist or psychiatrist is imperative.

Anxiety

Everybody feels tension. It's not only normal–it's a healthy emotional response to events in our lives that are troubling. When social pressures mount, so can our feelings of dread. When faced with a new task or limitation, our anxiety symptoms can escalate.

How one person feels anxiety is rarely how the next person will experience theirs. Some people are plagued by muscle tension in their shoulders or back while others get tension headaches. Some have stomach or bowel problems while others will shake and feel heart palpitations. Other symptoms of anxiety can include sleep loss, restlessness, excessive sweating, worry, and panic attacks that can mimic the feelings of a heart attack. While rarely physically debilitating, anxiety can nonetheless ruin somebody's day or life if left unaddressed.

Like depression, and so many other of life's challenges, the first step is in recognizing that something is wrong. There are normal, expected feelings of stress; but when those feelings begin to interfere with your life significantly, then recognizing and addressing them is key. A unique initial step to overcoming anxiety is to truly "feel" where inside your body you're being impacted. Don't own anxiety symptoms you don't have. (Oddly, Americans often "brag" about how stressed they are when they're barely feeling any discomfort at all.) Know your tension-related physical symptoms and become alerted to those symptoms when they begin, not hours or days later when you're immobile. Most people struggling with tension and stress can overcome their anxiety without medication; but in those very rare cases where one's anxiety is overwhelming, then talking with a psychiatrist may help. That said, please beware that virtually all anti-anxiety medications are highly addictive and you don't want to own the problem of addiction on top of the already-troubling problem of anxiety.

Psychosis

A fairly rare problem encountered as we age is psychosis. Being psychotic, whether short-term or life-long, usually presents a larger challenge, as it can negatively impact our social interactions, our self-care abilities, and our mental health far more pervasively than unhappiness and stress.

Psychosis, or "a departure from reality," often includes symptoms considered a bit more extreme or troubling to those suffering with it and those around them. Common symptoms can include hearing or seeing things that others don't; these are called "hallucinations," and they're usually very unpleasant or mean-spirited thoughts and images that can briefly interrupt one's breakfast or continue for days. The voices one hears are typically mean or sexualized or aggressive and bring about great worry and sorrow. Another common symptom of psychosis (which is often also called schizophrenia) is delusional, or unreal, thinking. Common delusional thoughts include paranoia regarding other people, highly-disorganized thinking, and/or feelings of ridiculous personal greatness and grandiosity.

Addressing psychosis, unlike feelings of depression or stress, is often best handled with the assistance of an experienced psychiatrist. While a talented therapist can often be an amazing resource, particularly with helping loved ones understand this mental illness, medications are often used to abate some of the more profound symptoms. However, these medications can have side effects, so careful monitoring is crucial. As with depression or anxiety, a person overwhelmed by schizophrenia may require mental health hospitalization to be stabilized. And as with depression or anxiety, this could be a life-long challenge that may wax and wane over time. Diligent recognition of one's own unique symptoms is imperative.

Substance Abuse

While one can often enjoy the occasional glass of wine or drinking beer with their friends with little or no negative problems, substance abuse among the elderly is a growing concern. Once hard-partying Baby Boomers are now entering their golden years and learning that lifestyles might need to change before mounting addictions take hold. Today's elderly, compared to just one generation before them, come from an era where alcohol and casual drug use was far more accepted. However, what might have been tolerated by your younger body or former social circle now portends a substance abuse problem that could be deadly.

Symptoms of substance abuse can include an inability cut down or stop use for even a day or two. Withdrawal symptoms such as nausea, headaches, or crabbiness can have a user hunting down more of their favorite intoxicant. Just because one can indulge in alcohol (or even marijuana) legally, doesn't mean it cannot destroy lives. When substance abuse is hidden or denied, the effects can be devastating. An addict can easily encounter problems with their families, their neighbors, their friends, or the law.

Obviously, the key to substance abuse is to not use the substance again, but that is often far more difficult than it sounds. Some substances, particularly alcohol, can be difficult to quit because it's everywhere. Still other substances are often prescribed by a physician and therefore come with some level of "imperative," even if little necessity exists. Also important is the risk of an annoying or painful withdrawal process, particularly if one's dependence has been on a "downer" such as alcohol, pain killers, or anti-anxiety medications. Getting off one's problematic substances might require the assistance of an experienced psychologist who specializes in substance abuse, a physician knowledgeable of all of the patient's assorted medications, or even a brief hospitalization to help with the initial detoxification.

Dementia

Often used interchangeably with the specific dementia process known as Alzheimer's disease, dementia generally refers to a profound loss of memory and all that goes along with it. Memory loss is a normal part of aging; and if you asked, most people would say they sometimes have a poor memory of things. But having a poor memory, whether later in life or life-long, is not to be confused with dementia. Like depression and anxiety, don't own it if you don't have it.

True dementia is a debilitating, typically uncurable, process of memory loss which starts with short-term losses and leads to the gradual loss of common skills and memories that rarely return. While some women may have complained their whole lives of misplacing their purses, misplacing your purse while it's dangling from your arm is a wholly different problem. Forgetting the name of your tenth grandchild is common; forgetting your own name is not. Other unfortunate symptoms of dementia include forgetting whether you took your medications or not, forgetting how to drive or get home, and even forgetting very basic life skills like how to bathe or eat or toilet oneself.

As dementia is both a psychological and biological concern, intervention can include both mental health professionals and physicians. While generally there is no "cure" in dementia, and one usually progresses from bad to worse, the progression can be better handled by family members who get support from others, learn from professionals in the field of geriatrics, and take care of themselves as caregivers. Caring for the caregiver is crucial, including eliciting support from additional family members and respite care. Often the difficult choice of placement, or professional in-home services, must be considered when the informal caregiving from loved ones is no longer adequate.

Get the Support You Need

The emotional problems of depression, anxiety, psychosis, substance abuse, or dementia are very challenging but need not be personally and permanently devastating. These psychological problems, often rooted in biological causes or the choices we've made, present us with challenges both minor and immense. As we age, these challenges often overlap and can feel overwhelming. For example, those who get anxious might begin to use drugs abundantly to overcome their stress. Dementia can bring about a spell of depression that can only make both problems worse. And there is a host of additional psychological problems not even mentioned that can worsen matters such as eating disorders, phobias, sexual problems, personality disorders, and so on.

The good news is that we are resilient creatures and forward movement is essential to who we are, and a mental health challenge might even lead to a blessing. Maybe the body is failing, but the mind is well; or perhaps the mind is failing, but the spirit is relieved.

Through suffering with a mental health dilemma, we may discover a social circle full of champions. There are few problems in our lives without solutions, particularly if one is willing to recognize and face those problems and armed with the support of others and the knowledge to do the right thing.

Notes

_____

_____

_____

_____

_____

_____

_____

_____

_____

_____

_____

_____

_____

_____

Notes

_____

_____

_____

_____

_____

_____

_____

_____

_____

_____

_____

_____

_____

_____

_____

_____

_____

_____

18

Alzheimer's and Dementia

ೞ

SERGIO CALDERÓN
MPH Associate VP, Alzheimer's Los Angeles

The gradual slipping away of mind and memory is frightening and frustrating, both for the person with the disease and for family and friends. It can elicit strong feelings of love, grief, anger, and exhaustion. My goal is to provide you with a basic understanding of Alzheimer's disease and where you can find free, tangible, resources to help you cope with the disease process.

Alzheimer's Disease & Related Dementias

"Alzheimer's (AHLZ-high-merz) is a disease of the brain that causes problems with memory, thinking, and behavior, and gets worse over time. Dementia (dih-MEN-shuh) is a general term used to describe the loss of memory and other intellectual abilities serious enough to interfere with daily life.

Although symptoms can vary widely, the first problem many people notice is forgetfulness severe enough to affect their ability to function at home or at work, or to enjoy lifelong hobbies. Other symptoms include confusion, getting lost in familiar places, misplacing things, and trouble with speaking or writing. Our brains change as we age, just like the rest of our bodies. However, serious memory loss, confusion, and other major changes in the way our minds work are not a normal part of aging.[3]"

In 1906, German neurologist and psychiatrist Dr. Alois Alzheimer described the case of Auguste D., a 51-year-old woman with a cluster of unusual symptoms, including problems with memory and comprehension, an inability to speak, behavioral problems, disorientation, and hallucinations. Upon examination of her brain tissue, Dr. Alzheimer described two of the hallmarks of Alzheimer's disease–numerous globs of sticky proteins in the spaces between neurons (beta-amyloid plaques) and a tangled bundle of fibrils within neurons (neurofibrillary tangles). Auguste

[3] Ronald Petersen, M.D., Ph.D., (2006). Mayo Clinic: Guide to Alzheimer's Disease. MN: Mayo Clinic Health Solutions.

D. is regarded as being the first case described by Alois Alzheimer to highlight the disease that would later carry his name.

Alzheimer's disease accounts for 50 to 70 percent of cases of dementia and is irreversible. Some facts:

- In the Inland Empire, which includes San Bernardino and Riverside Counties, the number of people living with Alzheimer's disease and related dementia is increasing rapidly due to the aging population. In 2015, it was 65,947 and is projected to climb to 116,707 by 2030–a 77% increase.

- High increases are anticipated among ethnic minorities due to population aging and increased burden of chronic disease, especially hypertension and diabetes.

- For most people living with Alzheimer's disease and related disorders, there are one to three people impacted by their care needs.

Many conditions can disrupt memory and mental function. Some conditions may cause temporary memory problems and may be reversible. They include depression, thyroid problems, certain infections/high fever, medication side effects, poor diet, delirium, excess use of alcohol, vitamin deficiencies, and head trauma/injury.

Is it Alzheimer's? If you have concerns about yourself or a loved one's memory loss, thinking skills, and behavior changes, you should consult a doctor. Your primary care physician must be involved in assessing the situation and may refer you to a specialist for further evaluation. If you need assistance finding a doctor with experience evaluating memory problems, Alzheimer's Los Angeles can help via our toll-free helpline at 844.435.7259.

An early diagnosis provides an opportunity for early intervention and can maximize a person's quality-of-life, decrease anxieties about the unknown cognitive changes in a person, allow more time to plan, and even benefit from treatment. Additionally, it is important for a physician to determine the cause of memory loss or other dementia-like symptoms, since some are reversible.

Communication

Communication is a basic human need. Both verbal and non-verbal behaviors signal our intent and purpose to reach out to others and connect with them to meet our basic needs. Caregivers must understand that this holds true for people-living with Alzheimer's disease or a related dementia. A person's quality-of-life is jeopardized if you take away this ability to connect. People living with Alzheimer's disease are still capable of communicating; however, as their disease progresses and their communication skills diminish, they require you to facilitate this ability and adapt or modify your communication style. Learning communication strategies is just as important to meeting a loved one's emotional, physical, and medical needs as is understanding the Alzheimer's disease process. Enhanced communication skills can facilitate meeting the needs of the person living with dementia and may help alleviate caregiver stress and the burden of caregiving. A caregiver's role is to change and adjust their approach when communicating to the person living with the disease and join in their reality. Remember, "when they can no longer join us in our world, we must join them in theirs." Anonymous

Alzheimer's Los Angeles recommends the following to make your communication with your loved one more effective:

Do's

- Give short, one-sentence explanations.
- Allow plenty of time for comprehension, and then triple it.
- Repeat instructions or sentences exactly the same way.
- Eliminate "but" from your vocabulary; substitute "nevertheless."
- Avoid insistence. Try again later.
- Agree with them or distract them to a different subject or activity.
- Accept the blame when something's wrong (even if it's fantasy).
- Leave the room, if necessary, to avoid confrontations.
- Respond to the feelings rather than the words.
- Be patient and cheerful and reassuring. Go with the flow.
- Practice 100% forgiveness. Memory loss progresses daily.
- Elevate your level of generosity and graciousness.

Don't

- Don't argue.
- Don't remind them they forget.
- Don't try to reason with them.
- Don't question recent memory.
- Don't confront.
- Don't take it personally.

Strategies for Dealing with Challenging Behaviors

The progressive destruction of brain cells affects individuals in various stages of Alzheimer's disease differently, causing impairment that goes beyond their memory and other cognitive processes, including the way they feel and act. The stage of dementia, the location in the brain of the brain cell destruction, and various other factors can cause behavioral and psychological symptoms in a person living with dementia.

Behaviors that pose a challenge may be related to a physical discomfort, over-stimulation, an unfamiliar surrounding or frustrating interaction, or being asked to perform complicated tasks. Remember that the person living with Alzheimer's disease and related dementias has a neurological disease that causes progressive cognitive decline and decreases their ability to interpret, understand, and manage the internal and external stimuli they receive. Below is a sample of the symptoms that may be experienced–the most challenging and distressing effects of Alzheimer's disease:

- Physical or verbal outbursts
- General emotional distress
- Restlessness, pacing, shredding paper or tissues, and yelling
- Hallucinations (seeing, hearing, or feeling things that are not really there)
- Delusions (firmly held belief in things that are not real)

There are two approaches to managing behavioral symptoms: Using medications to control the symptoms or non-drug, non-pharmaceutical strategies. Non-drug approaches should always be tried first and include recognition that the person is not "acting mean or ornery," but is having further symptoms of the disease. The person living with Alzheimer's is not intentionally trying to behave a certain way, nor is their behavior a choice. Understanding that there are variables to the cause of behavioral and psychological symptoms of dementia can help family caregivers adjust their approach to dementia care.

A three-step approach to help identify common behaviors and their causes includes Alzheimer's Los Angeles' *IDEA! Strategy* see below.

You can find this Caregiver Tip Sheet and other Tip Sheets at: www.ALZLA.org

IDEA! Strategy

An approach to help you figure out why a behavior is happening and what you can do about it.

IDentify the behavior

- What is the behavior that is difficult for you to deal with? Be specific.
- Can you see it? Does it bother others? When does it happen? Who's around when it occurs?

Explore what may be causing the behavior

Understand the cause of the behavior

- **HEALTH:** Is the person taking a new medication, getting sick, or in pain?
- **ENVIRONMENT:** Is it too noisy? Is it too hot? Is the place unfamiliar?
- **TASK:** Is the activity too hard for them now? Are there too many steps? Is it something new?
- **COMMUNICATION:** Is it hard for the person to understand what you are saying?

Understand the meaning of the behavior to the person

- Does the person feel confused, scared, nervous, unhappy, or bored?
- Does the person feel like they are being treated like a child?
- Are there things that remind the person of something that they used to do when they were younger like go to work or pick up the children from school?

Adjust what can be done

You are the one who will need to change, the person cannot. Try different things. Pay attention to the person's feelings. Practice being calm, gentle, and reassuring.

- address what is causing the behavior
  - keep tasks and activities simple
  - keep the home as calm as possible
  - speak slowly and gently — try not to say too much at once
  - do not argue — agree and comfort the person whether they are right or wrong
  - find meaningful, simple activities so the person isn't bored
- distract or redirect by:
  - offering something they like to eat
  - watching a TV show or listening to music
  - asking for their help with a simple activity
  - leading them to a different room
- accept the behavior
  - some behaviors you may need to accept rather than change
  - if there are no safety concerns and it doesn't bother the person, you may need to find ways to live with it

Alzheimer's
LOS ANGELES
844.HELP.ALZ
AlzheimersLA.org
© 2018. Alzheimer's Los Angeles
Supported by DHHS, ACL (#90AL0003-01-00)

Estrategia ¡IDEA!

Una manera para ayudarle a descubrir porque ciertos comportamientos ocurren y que puede hacer al respecto.

IDentifique el comportamiento

- ¿Cuál es el comportamiento más difícil de lidiar para usted? Sea específico.
- ¿Lo puede ver? ¿Le molesta a otros? ¿Cuándo sucede? ¿Quién está cerca cuando sucede?

Entienda que podría estar causando el comportamiento

Entendiendo la causa del comportamiento

- **SALUD:** ¿Está tomando un nuevo medicamento? ¿Estará enfermándose? ¿Le dolerá algo?
- **AMBIENTE:** ¿Hay mucho ruido? ¿Hace mucho calor? ¿Está en un lugar desconocido?
- **ACTIVIDAD:** ¿Será que la actividad ahora es muy difícil para ellos, aunque antes lo hacían sin problema? ¿Tendrá muchos pasos? ¿Es algo nuevo?
- **COMUNICACIÓN:** ¿Será que la persona está teniendo problemas para entender lo que usted le está diciendo?

Entendiendo el significado del comportamiento para la persona

- ¿Estará confundido, asustado, nervioso, triste, o aburrido?
- ¿Sentirá que usted lo está tratando como si fuera niño?
- ¿Habrá cosas que le recuerden la persona de algo de cuando era joven, como de cuando iba a trabajar, o recoger a los niños de la escuela?

Adapte lo que se pueda hacer

Usted será el que tiene que cambiar. La persona no puede cambiar. Pruebe cosas diferentes. Ponga atención a los sentimientos de la persona. Practique manteniendo la calma, sea amable, y tranquilice a la persona.

- dirija su atención a lo que puede estar causando el comportamiento
  - mantenga las tareas y actividades sencillas
  - mantenga el hogar lo más calmado posible
  - hable lentamente y con calma — trate de no dar mucha información a la vez
  - no discuta — déle la razón y consuele a la persona sin importar si está equivocada o no
  - encuentre actividades significativas y sencillas para que la persona no se aburra
- distráigalo:
  - ofreciéndole algo que le guste de comer
  - viendo la televisión o escuchando música
  - pidiéndole que le ayude con una actividad simple, como doblar las toallas
  - llévelo a otro cuarto
- acepte el comportamiento
  - hay algunos comportamientos que se tendrán que aceptar en lugar de tratar de cambiarlos
  - si no causan problemas de seguridad y no molestan a la persona, entonces usted debe encontrar formas de vivir con el comportamiento

Alzheimer's
LOS ANGELES
844.HELP.ALZ
AlzheimersLA.org
© 2018 Alzheimer's Los Angeles
Supported by DHHS, ACL (90ALGG0027-01-00)

Get the Support You Need

A family caregiver is in the best position to help the person living with Alzheimer's or a related dementia when they are experiencing a behavioral and psychological symptom of dementia. Alzheimer's Los Angeles encourages family caregivers to learn as much as possible about the disease and develop their skills to learn how to modify the care recipient's environment, analyze potential causes/triggers or possible reinforcers, and how to adjust their approach and response to the behavioral and psychological symptoms of dementia.

Call Alzheimer's Los Angeles to explore non-drug approaches to dementia-care, including the *Savvy Caregiver Program* (*Savvy*)–a six-week, evidence-based, psycho-educational intervention with proven benefits to family caregivers. Take advantage of our *Memory Club* and *Grad Club*–weekly comprehensive support, education, and peer groups for people with early stage memory loss and their care partners. Or call our professional care counselor, that is bilingual and bicultural, who assists family caregivers by providing support, training, counseling, and help linking with needed services. Connect with our caregiver and community education programs offered in a variety of languages. Some of these programs are funded by the County of Riverside, Office on Aging, and other local funders.

Being a caregiver is a big responsibility, and you need to keep things in perspective. It is important that caregivers maintain balance, acknowledge their emotions, and ask for help when needed, don't wait. Our aim at Alzheimer's Los Angeles is to provide you family-centered care; we know Alzheimer's is tough and we'd like to face it together. Again, call Alzheimer's Los Angeles to get free supportive-services and help by calling the toll-free helpline at 844.435.7259.

Alzheimer's Los Angeles hopes that the information provided proves to be helpful and that you access the resources listed. Call Alzheimer's Los Angeles at 844.435.7259 to seek additional free help. We encourage families to get involved as an advocate and perhaps volunteer with us or join the international US Against Alzheimer's movement to raise funds to progress Alzheimer's disease research.

Alzheimer's Disease is Tough
Let's Face it Together

Toll-free Helpline:
1.844.435.7259 (toll free)

Linea de Ayuda:
1.844.435.7259

Inland Empire Office:
1.951.241.7878

http://www.alzla.org

Sources

Alzheimer's Los Angeles, (2018). Brochure: Helping Families.

Alzheimer's Los Angeles, (2018/2019). Caregiver Tip Sheets/ Hojas de consejos para el cuidador. www.ALZLA.org

National Institute on Aging, (2008). Alzheimer's Disease: Unraveling the Mystery.

Susan Kohler. How to Communicate with Alzheimer's: A practical guide and workbook for families.

Frank Broyles, (2006). Coach Broyles' Playbook for Alzheimer's Caregivers: A practical tips guide.

USAgainstAlzheimer's.org

Communication (2008). Liz Ayres, Alzheimer's Orange County

Notes

Notes

19

The Latest in Alzheimer's Research

ଓଃ

KRYSTLE JOSEPH
Alzheimer's Association

More than 100 years have passed since German physician Dr. Alois Alzheimer first discovered the amyloid plaques and tau tangles in the brain that characterize Alzheimer's disease. However, only in the last 35 years has research into the causes, treatments, symptoms, and risk factors of Alzheimer's gained momentum.

The Alzheimer's Association has undertaken several research initiatives in anticipation of the escalating number of individuals who will develop Alzheimer's disease as the baby boomer generation ages, and in recognition of the need to make up for lost time.

For decades, the behavioral changes and decline in thinking abilities associated with Alzheimer's disease were believed by many to be a normal part of aging, so research into the disease was limited. As time passed, this perception eventually changed. With this came awareness that Alzheimer's is impacting not only the individuals with the disease, but also their caregivers and families, and–with the care and support services required as the disease progresses–society as a whole.

The statistics on the disease will stop you in your tracks. Alzheimer's disease is currently the 6th leading cause of death in the United States. Every 65 seconds, someone in the U.S. develops the disease, while 5.8 million Americans are currently living with Alzheimer's. By 2050, this number is projected to rise to nearly 14 million.

We also saw that between 2000 and 2017, deaths from heart disease have decreased 9%, while deaths from Alzheimer's disease have increased 145%. The growth of Alzheimer's disease and other dementias are a mounting global health crisis. In 2019,

Alzheimer's and other dementias will cost the nation $290 billion; by 2050, these costs could rise as high as $1.1 trillion.

In order to solve this global health crisis, there is an immediate need for better treatment, earlier detection, and strategies focusing on prevention–all of which is the focus of Alzheimer's disease research.

Some other items to note about the disease:

- We know that currently-approved Alzheimer's drugs, while helpful to some, are unsatisfactory. They do not change the course of the disease, though they do provide some symptomatic relief to some.

- There is a need for understanding the basic biology underlying Alzheimer's disease, including how our brain cells work and what goes wrong when a person has Alzheimer's.

- The Alzheimer's research field is developing new technologies to detect Alzheimer's earlier.

- Using advanced imaging, such as PET scans, we can now see Alzheimer's-related changes in living people up to 20 years before clinical symptoms of cognitive decline.

- Emerging diagnostics such as cerebrospinal fluid analysis, blood tests, saliva analysis, and optical evaluation are in development as tools for early Alzheimer's detection.

Ultimately, early and accurate diagnosis are critical to ensure that people receive high-quality care and can plan for the future. It also enables enrollment in clinical trials at the earliest stages of disease, when effective treatment and prevention may still be possible.

A Deeper Look at the latest in Research: AAIC 2019 Synopsis

The Alzheimer's Association International Conference® (AAIC®) is the world's largest gathering of Alzheimer's and dementia researchers. Through this annual conference, the Association aims to foster the information sharing and collaboration among scientists that is essential to accelerating progress toward the association's vision of a world without Alzheimer's.

This year's conference was held in July 2019 in Los Angeles and featured promising and hopeful reports from scientific studies that used diverse approaches to uncover the causes, progression, risk factors, treatment, and prevention of Alzheimer's and other dementias.

Bringing the world closer to breakthroughs in dementia science, AAIC 2019 convened nearly 6,000 leading experts and researchers from around the world and featured more than 3,400 scientific presentations. More than 100 leading philanthropists attended as part of the Global Immersion Experience.

The key takeaways from this conference are important for every caregiver to know.

1. **Lifestyle Interventions Can Offset Elevated Alzheimer's Risk**

   New research reported at AAIC 2019 suggests that making multiple healthy lifestyle choices, including healthy diet, not smoking, regular exercise, and cognitive stimulation, may decrease the risk of cognitive decline and dementia. One study reported that participants who adopted four or five low-risk lifestyle factors had about 60% lower risk of Alzheimer's dementia compared with participants who did not follow any or only one of the low-risk factors.

Two studies showed that actionable lifestyle changes could potentially counteract elevated risk for Alzheimer's disease. In one report, researchers showed that participants with a high genetic risk for Alzheimer's following a "favorable" lifestyle had a 32% lower risk of all-cause dementia compared with an "unfavorable" lifestyle. Another report confirmed that living in locations with high air pollution increased the risk for Alzheimer's and other dementias. However, it also found that older women with higher cognitive reserve–based on cognitive function scores, years of education, job status, and physical activity–showed only a 21% increased environmental risk compared with a 113% increased risk for those with lower cognitive reserve.

The bottom line is that healthy eating, regular exercise, and cognitive stimulation is important for you and your loved one to decrease the risk of Alzheimer's.

2. **Blood Markers Could Improve Diagnosis of Alzheimer's**

Data presented at AAIC 2019 described advances in blood-based methods for evaluating biological markers of Alzheimer's and other neurodegenerative diseases, such as abnormal versions of amyloid protein as well as alpha synuclein (dementia with Lewy Bodies) and neurofilament light (general brain cell damage). There is a great need for reliable, inexpensive, easy to administer, non-invasive, and easily available diagnostic tools for Alzheimer's. Families facing Alzheimer's now and in the future would benefit greatly from tools that could accelerate diagnosis earlier in the disease process and allow for improved and accelerated delivery of care and planning. These new testing technologies, which are currently under development by industry and academic researchers, could potentially be used to track the impact of therapies in clinical trials as well.

3. **Alzheimer's Risk, Progression and Resilience Differs by Sex**

Researchers at AAIC 2019 reported having identified several differences in the biology, progression and risk of Alzheimer's disease between men and women. Four studies reported on sex-specific differences that could inform unique risk profiles and help the field better understand why the majority of people living with Alzheimer's are women.

Two studies found 11 novel sex-specific risk genes for Alzheimer's disease, as well as differences in the structural and functional connections in the brains of women that might contribute to the accelerated spread of abnormal tau protein, which tracks closely with cognitive decline in Alzheimer's and other dementias. Another study suggests that women have higher levels of brain energy usage than men, potentially explaining women's better verbal memory and better compensation for early Alzheimer's-related brain changes. A fourth study found that women who participated in the paid labor force between early adulthood and middle age showed slower rates of memory decline in late-life compared with those who did not engage in waged employment.

If you're a woman or taking care of your mother, keep flexing that brain power.

4. **New Alzheimer's Clinical Trials Test Novel Treatment Approaches**

At AAIC 2019, researchers reported 18-month results from the open-label extension of the SNIFF trial, a Phase 2/3 trial evaluating the use of intranasal insulin for people with mild cognitive impairment or Alzheimer's disease. The study found that, for a group of just over 40 participants who used the original drug delivery device, those treated with insulin had significantly better cognitive and functional test scores compared with those who received a placebo. However, this was not observed in a group that used a different intranasal delivery device. While encouraging, follow-up studies are needed.

Other researchers reported on the initiation of the GAIN trial, a large Phase 2/3 study in mild to moderate Alzheimer's. The study is the first large, international trial to evaluate a therapeutic approach based on emerging data that suggest the bacterium Porphyromonas gingivalis, commonly associated with gum disease, can infect the brain and lead to Alzheimer's disease. The GAIN trial has begun enrolling 570 patients in the United States and Europe.

5. Expert Panel Discusses Role of Infectious Agents in Alzheimer's Disease

AAIC 2019 hosted a panel in which several experts in the field shared differing views on the role of infectious agents in Alzheimer's. Two scientists explained and defended the hypothesis that the herpes virus may be a causative factor for the disease, perhaps involving brain inflammation or a reduced immune system. One researcher suggested that immune response to bacterial infection in the brain may start a cascade that leads to well-known brain changes, including the formation of amyloid plaques–the hallmark brain lesions of Alzheimer's. He suggested that amyloid beta protein protects the brain against infection by entrapping invading microbes within amyloid deposits. Two scientists questioned key aspects of the microbial hypothesis of Alzheimer's, even expressing concern that it "may distract the field from more impactful research."

Prevention Trials–US POINTER STUDY

The U.S. Study to Protect Brain Health Through Lifestyle Intervention to Reduce Risk (U.S. POINTER) is a two-year clinical trial to evaluate whether lifestyle interventions that simultaneously target multiple risk factors protect cognitive function in older adults (age 60-79) at increased risk for cognitive decline. The multisite randomized clinical trial will investigate whether exercise, nutrition, and other health-related changes can impact older adults who are at risk. The U.S. POINTER study is now active at four sites in the U.S. with a fifth launching soon. Philanthropic supporters have given nearly $8 million to date to enable this five-year, $35 million study.

In addition to funding from the Alzheimer's Association, the U.S. National Institute on Aging (NIA) has recently awarded a five-year $47 million grant to the University of California, Berkeley, to incorporate imaging into this ongoing study investigating whether lifestyle changes can help protect against dementia.

The $47 million grant from the NIA, part of the National Institutes of Health, will go toward the Neuroimaging Ancillary Study, which intends to use brain imaging methods to assess how such lifestyle changes impact brain health.

"A healthy diet and lifestyle are generally recognized as good for health, but this study is the first large randomized controlled trial to look at whether lifestyle changes actually influence Alzheimer's disease-related brain changes," Susan Landau, a research neuroscientist at Berkeley's Helen Wills Neuroscience Institute and principal investigator of the add-on study, said in a prepared statement.

According to the statement, MRI will be used to monitor overall and regional brain shape, size, and blood flow and indicators of vascular disease that impact the brains of study participants. PET scanning will be employed to assess beta-amyloid buildup and tau proteins in the brain.

"U.S. POINTER is designed to determine what lifestyle interventions have a tangible impact on our brains," said Maria C. Carrillo, PhD, chief science officer of the Alzheimer's Association, which is sponsoring the study. "The addition of brain imaging is an important component that could provide the roadmap for brain health to reduce the risk of dementia before symptoms have a chance to appear."

Learn more by visiting: https://www.alz.org/us-pointer

Clinical Trials and TrialMatch

Clinical trials are the engine that powers medical progress. Through clinical trials, researchers test new ways to detect, treat, and prevent Alzheimer's disease and related dementias. Without clinical trials, there can be no new treatments or cures. TrialMatch is a free service that makes it easy for people with Alzheimer's, caregivers, families, and physicians to locate clinical trials based on personal criteria (diagnosis, stage of disease) and location.

Alzheimer's Association TrialMatch holds over 300 clinical trials related to Alzheimer's disease and other dementias that need cognitively healthy participants as well as participants with MCI, Alzheimer's, and other dementias.

The Association created TrialMatch because recruiting and retaining participants for clinical studies is one of the greatest obstacles to developing the next generation of Alzheimer's treatments. The immediate need for advances in diagnosis, treatment, and prevention has led to an unprecedented call for clinical study participants.

By volunteering for clinical studies, people living with Alzheimer's and their caregivers can play a more active role in their own treatment while also contributing to scientific discovery and benefiting future generations. It is public service in the best possible sense.

As constituents become more knowledgeable and curious about Alzheimer's research, having a program like TrialMatch is critical to achieving our vision of a world without Alzheimer's disease.

To learn more about TrialMatch, visit: www.alz.org/trialmatch

In Conclusion

Overall, this is a very exciting time in Alzheimer's disease research:

- Tremendous gains have been made in understanding of the basic biology underlying Alzheimer's disease, including how brain cells work and what goes wrong in Alzheimer's.

- Great strides have been made in developing tests to detect Alzheimer's disease.

- We've seen promise in lifestyle interventions to slow cognitive decline and maybe dementia.

With the proper investment in funding, we will see an accelerated pace of discovery to slow, stop, and ultimately prevent Alzheimer's disease.

Federal funding is at an all-time high. Including a $425 million increase for fiscal year 2019, Alzheimer's and dementia research funding at the National Institutes of Health is now $2.3 billion annually. Since the passage of the National Alzheimer's Project Act, the Congress has more than quadrupled Alzheimer's research.

In addition, the Alzheimer's Association has awarded more than $455 million to nearly 3,000 best-of-field grant proposals since awarding its first grants in 1982, and is the world's largest nonprofit funder of Alzheimer's disease research. In 2018 alone, more than $30 million was awarded in grant funding to over 131 scientific investigations.

These unprecedented levels of philanthropic investment and federal funding in Alzheimer's research enable scientists to work at a more rapid pace to advance basic knowledge about Alzheimer's, explore ways to reduce risk, uncover new biomarkers for early diagnosis and drug targeting, and develop potential treatments.

For more information on upcoming research progress:

- *Alzheimer's & Dementia: The Journal of the Alzheimer's Association* is a monthly, peer-reviewed journal that aims to bridge knowledge gaps separating traditional fields of dementia research by covering the entire spectrum from basic science to clinical trials and social and behavioral investigations. The Association also has two online-only journals: Alzheimer's & Dementia: Diagnosis, Assessment & Disease Monitoring and Alzheimer's & Dementia: Translational Research & Clinical Interventions.

- Stay tuned for the 2020 Alzheimer's Association International Conference, July 25-27 in Amsterdam: https://www.alz.org/aaic

JOIN THE FIGHT FOR ALZHEIMER'S FIRST SURVIVOR.

Notes

_____

_____

_____

_____

_____

_____

_____

_____

_____

_____

_____

_____

_____

_____

_____

_____

Notes

20

Holistic Health for the Elderly

ℭ𝔰

KRIS WOODS
Registered Nurse

Care of an elderly parent or loved one can be challenging even for the most dedicated caregivers. Problems associated with aging run the gamut of social, emotional, mental, physical, and even spiritual–in a word "holistic," from the Greek root meaning "whole." Regardless of the challenges faced by your aging parent(s), you can offer a measure of hope and healing by helping them meet their health challenges in the most practical and economical way through a system of healing we call Naturopathy.

Naturopathy, or 'nature cure' therapy, was coined during the early part of the last century by pioneers of alternative medicine. It describes living by natural law and using nature's gift to maintain and restore health. While medicine's job is to diagnose disease and treat symptoms, naturopaths believe that the body has an innate ability to heal if we bring it back into balance through right living.

It is my personal belief that healing is best done using natural remedies whenever possible and reserving medicine for life-threatening illness or disease. My hope is that in reading this chapter, you will be compelled to learn more about the many modalities available in complementary medicine that will assist you in improving the health and quality of life for your aging parent.

The Challenges of Aging

As we age, our body's ability to self-regulate and repair becomes diminished; and while decline is inevitable, there are many interventions available that can slow or offset the negative effects of aging. Let's examine some of the physiological effects that aging brings:

- **Immune System:** Diminished immune function can lead to increased infections, autoimmune diseases, and cancer.

- **Glandular System:** Decreased production of glandular secretions, such as enzymes and hormones, impact vital organs' abilities to function.

- **Circulation:** Hardened or plagued arteries decrease vein integrity causing poor circulation. In addition, the body's production of red and white blood cells is diminished.

- **Digestion/Excretion:** Decreased stomach acid and enzyme production impede proper digestion and diminished bowel motility, which can lead to malnutrition and constipation.

- **Kidney/Bladder:** Decreased kidney function as a result of hardened arteries and veins can lead to toxic buildup in the system. Loss of bladder tone increases the risk for urinary tract infections.

- **Nervous System:** Diminished nerve activity results in slower reflexes and nerve insensitivity. Decline in the autonomic nervous system impedes the functioning of vital organs.

- **Structural System:** Weakened bones and muscles result in breakage and deformities, leading to pain, stiffness, and loss of mobility.

By adhering to some simple guidelines of natural healing, you can assist your loved one to mitigate, and even reverse, many of the problems associated with aging.

Principles of Health and Healing

Health begins with right living and taking a holistic approach by nourishing our bodies, our minds, and our spirits. Understanding the issues that directly affect health, you can assist your loved one by recognizing areas in their lives that may need adjusting. While it has been said that the older we get, the more resistant we are to change, I have found that by gently coaxing senior adults through education and common-sense reasoning, it is easier to get them to mend their unhealthy habits. My experience has shown that small changes positively impact how people feel each day and encourage them to continue making better choices for their health.

Fresh Air and Sunshine

The best source of fresh air is outside and away from heavy traffic. If your parent is agile enough, he/she may enjoy taking up golf or croquet. Walking is an excellent outdoor activity for any age, as it keeps the bones and muscles strong and improves circulation. You may be able to interest your loved one in gardening, another activity than many people enjoy. If mobility is a problem, you might explore container gardening, where plants can be maintained in raised beds or pots so that less stooping and bending is required. Even wheelchair-bound persons can enjoy the outdoors, regardless of the activity. Of course, safety should always be the first concern.

Sunshine is so important, not only because of the life-enhancing energy that the sun provides, but because of its ability to stimulate the production Vitamin D. This vitamin is necessary for the utilization of calcium in building strong teeth and bones. Vitamin D also improves our immune function, which can prevent many illnesses, such as colds and flu, and even cancer. Vitamin D is also an important vitamin for minimizing depression, a common problem for many older adults. Because seniors have very sensitive skin, protection from harsh sunlight is important. A large brim hat and sunglasses should be worn to keep the sun off of the face and out of sensitive eyes. Exposing the arms, legs, or larger areas of the body to the sun is less harmful. Ten to fifteen minutes of early morning or late afternoon sun (between 3:00 and 4:00 pm) is adequate for older adults.

Activity and Hygiene

Active adults seem to have less illness and disease than non-active ones. Our bodies were meant to move. Since we no longer have to gather and hunt for our food, we have become accustomed to activities that do not require much physical activity. Many retired seniors spend a lot of time watching television. While this provides a measure of leisure and comfort, it does not allow them to enjoy the social connections that they need to stay mentally active, and it does little to keep their circulation moving or their bones and muscles strong. Encourage your loved one to engage in activities that keep them physically active. Find a senior center in their area where there are programs and activities that encourage physical, social, and mental stimulation.

It's also important to recognize the healing effects of water and hygiene for maintaining health. While bathing each day may not be necessary for older or inactive adults, personal hygiene is vital.

Many seniors enjoy warm showers, and if your loved one is agile enough, this can be done safely. Make sure that the shower has a rubber mat to prevent slipping and grab bars in and along the shower that they can hold to stabilize themselves and to maneuver safely. While immersing the body in water is the ideal way to bath, older adults cannot accomplish this safely enough in a bathtub. If your loved one is bed or chair bound, bathing can still be accomplished by a "bed bath." A warm washcloth to the face and neck, arms and hands, legs and feet will bring circulation to the skin's surface, helping to expel toxins and hydrate the tissues. Soap may not be necessary and in fact may be too harsh on older, sensitive skin; but a non-mineral oil-based lotion or cream keeps the skin moist and supple and may prevent some skin diseases. The genital area should be washed gently with a mild, antibiotic soap to kill bacteria and fungus. This is especially important if your loved one is incontinent of urine or stool. Immobility, poor circulation, and poor hygiene are three main reasons that many immobile adults experience skin breakdown. Decubitus ulcers ("bedsores") are a leading cause of morbidity and mortality in the geriatric population, and scrupulous attention to the skin is paramount in preventing skin problems.

Mental Health and Stress Management

Change is hard for many people and, in particular, aging seniors. Loss of friends and loved ones, financial worries, failing health, and other stresses put an enormous strain on the elderly, resulting in depression and loss of quality of life. Depression affects more than 6 million Americans over the age of 65. Suicide rates among adults over 80 are higher than any other age group.[11]

Depression is NOT a normal part of aging, and can be managed through nutrition and life-style changes, as well as medical intervention when necessary. It can be expected that death of a spouse will cause grieving and even temporary depression. But if grieving continues for a prolonged period of time, symptoms of depression should be taken very seriously. Symptoms may include loss of interest in normal activities that previously provided pleasure; loss of appetite and weight loss; inability to sleep, or sleeping for long periods during the day, and frequent illnesses. For more information on the causes and signs/symptoms of Depression, refer to Office of Aging website.[9]

Let Food Be Your Medicine

It may come as no surprise to many people that poor nutrition plays an important part in overall health. One of the most recognized symptoms of poor nutrition is depression. Why? Because without certain nutrients, our brains cannot make chemicals that help maintain mood. These chemicals are called neurotransmitters. They are messenger chemicals that relay information from one cell to another throughout our nervous system. Neurotransmitters are very important chemicals that control mood, appetite, sleep, and mental function, to name a few. In order for our bodies to make neurotransmitters, we need to eat a variety of whole foods each day and to supplement with nutrients that we can't always get in our diets.

> *"Let food be thy medicine and let medicine be thy food."*
> *– Hippocrates*

Hippocrates, the "Father of Modern Medicine," understood more than 2500 years ago the connection between a nutritious diet and health. Today, we know much more about the science of nutrition and its impact on health. In order to thrive, grow, reproduce, build and repair, our bodies need basic nutritional ingredients: proteins, fats (lipids), carbohydrates, vitamins, minerals, enzymes, and phytonutrients (plant chemicals). Helping to keep your aging parent healthy may mean assisting them to choose nutritious foods and to prepare them in healthy and tasteful ways. Shopping for foods that "could be found in the Garden of Eden" is one of the best visuals I have used to help clients understand where to shop in the grocery store. Eating "manmade" foods that are loaded with artificial ingredients and preservatives should only be used as a last choice, if the goal is eating for one's health.

Proteins

A healthy diet consists of foods rich in the basic food groups, with an emphasis on fresh vegetables, fruits, and high-protein plant foods. High quality *proteins* help our bodies build strong muscles, bones and nerves and also maintain our hormone levels, among many other functions. Some of the better-quality proteins are found in such foods as:

- Brown beans and legumes, such as peas and lentils

- Lean meats, such as chicken and fish, pork and turkey

- Organic dairy products such as low-fat milk, buttermilk, yogurt, cheese, butter and eggs

- Whole grains and brown rice

- Raw nuts such as walnuts, almonds and pecans

Carbohydrates

We also need energy to carry on complex chemical processes and energy comes from *carbohydrates*. Carbohydrate foods break down into a sugar called glucose which we need for energy. The healthiest sources of carbohydrates come from plants–specifically fruits and vegetables. Scientists have discovered that the colors of fruits and vegetables are created by the health enhancing chemicals that are in these plants. Choose from a large selection, such as:

- Green, red, and yellow peppers

- Tomatoes

- Garlic and onions

- Squashes

- Carrots, yams, and sweet potatoes

- Green beans and peas

- Herbs and spices (fresh or dried)

- Apples, pears, and grapes

- Tropical fruits such as pineapples, mangos, and papayas

- Bananas

- Citrus fruits such as oranges, lemons, grapefruit, and melon

- All colors of berries

Fats

Our bodies need fats called *lipids*. Lipids are made of essential fatty acids that are used by our bodies to perform many functions, like protecting our cells from damage; helping cells communicate with other cells; energy storage; lowering cholesterol; alleviating stiffness and joint pain; fighting depression; keeping skin smooth and supple; and maybe even helping fight off Alzheimer's and dementia. Healthy fats can be found in many varieties of nuts and seeds, which can be mashed or ground and incorporated into many recipes.

- Raw nuts and seeds
- Avocados
- Olives
- Olive and nut oils
- Flax seeds & flax seed oil
- Wheat germ
- Coconut and coconut oil

Water

In addition to a healthy diet, drinking plenty of water is good for everyone, but especially as we age. Water is essential for clear thinking, healthy skin, good circulation, heart health, improve kidney and bowel function, as well as preventing bladder infections. Not a fan of water? Try herbal teas, a great addition to any diet that provides not just water, but essential nutrients and healing plant oils. Adding fruits, like lemon, strawberries, blueberries to water enhances flavor. Many adults enjoy a warm cup of tea–even in the summer!

Nutritional Supplements

Getting all the nutrients we need each day is difficult enough, but for seniors who have health issues that impact nutrition, it is especially hard. Nutritional supplements can be found in tablet/

capsule or liquid form these days, and many nutritional drinks offer essential nutrients described below. (Look for drinks with low sugar content.) In addition to a healthy diet, I use and recommend the following nutritional supplements for my clients as a minimum to take each day:

- A whole food vitamin and mineral supplement
- Flax seed oil, either in liquid or capsule form
- Digestive enzymes to improve food assimilation
- Probiotics to maintain a healthy digestive tract
- A fiber supplement, in addition to dietary fiber

A Word About Food Labeling

It's so important to read labels on all food products, as there are many ingredients in processed foods that are actually harmful to our health, often by interfering with vital cellular processes. High fructose corn syrup–an extremely concentrated sweetener–is especially harmful for older adults in that the aging body is not able to clear sugar as well as when we are young. This puts an enormous stress on the pancreas, as well as the cells of the entire body including the brain. Because Type II Diabetes is rampant in aging adults, eliminating all sources of 'unnatural' sugars is very important. While it may be difficult to find foods that do not have high fructose corn syrup (HFCS) in them, many companies are beginning to bend to customer demand for healthier food products, and many products on the shelves today are free of this harmful ingredient.

Another food additive that disrupts the body's cellular activity is *hydrogenated oils*, also known as "transfats." Transfats are oils that have been processed to prolong shelf life of processed foods, but are oils that actually shorten *our* lives! Not only do transfats interfere with the absorption of essential fat-soluble vitamins, they cause an inflammatory response in the body, a key to the development of illness and chronic disease.

Chemicals additives and food colorings do little to improve health. Most are added for enhanced taste and eye appeal. One harmful ingredient that many people recognize is MSG (monosodium glutamate). MSG is hidden in foods under many label ingredients that you may recognize: "hydrolyzed vegetable protein," "stock," and "natural flavoring" are examples. Dr. Russell Blaylock, a renowned neurosurgeon who has studied the effects of food additives on our brains for many years, implicates many of these food additives in the growing incidence of Alzheimer's and other dementias in our aging population. He cautions against buying any foods that have what he describes as "excitotoxins" in them.[7]

The fewer ingredients you see on any food label, the better. If you shop for or with your parent, make them aware that the best foods have no label at all—just as God created them! Most elderly people do not read labels (for one, labels are VERY hard to read!), choosing instead to purchase foods that don't stretch their fixed budgets. There IS a way to shop for healthier foods without breaking the bank, and you can be the best resource for helping your loved one accomplish this. Preparing fresh foods at home is always the best option. If your parents do not live with you, they will always be appreciative if you bring homemade foods when you visit!

Natural Remedies for Age Related Disorders

There are many safe, natural, cost-effective, and convenient ways to improve health and mitigate the symptoms of many diseases of aging. While I never discourage the use of medications, it has been my experience that using drugs as a first line of defense for non-life-threatening illnesses often causes more problems than it cures. Keep in mind that drugs work relatively quickly, but natural methods take more time. A general guideline is to allow a month of healing for each year a problem has been manifesting. Here are some general guidelines for common ailments:

- **Arthritis:** Arthritis is inflammation of the joints. The main symptom is pain, and this can often be debilitating. The key to mitigating arthritis pain and stiffness is to reduce or eliminate the inflammation. One of the best ways to accomplish this is through a healthy diet. A vegetable-based diet will provide the nutrients necessary for the repair of joints. Adequate fluid intake will help move fluid and toxins out of the joints, which will improve mobility and pain. My clients who take adequate amounts of flax seed oil each day often report less pain or complete remission of their arthritis symptoms. Flax Oil can be added to vegetables after steaming, used as a base for salad dressings, or mixed into hot cereals. It has a light, nutty flavor that many people find agreeable. Keep flax oil refrigerated for longer shelf life, and never take flax oils that are bitter or rancid. Two other supplements that many people swear by for improving arthritis are Glucosamine and Chondroitin. They should be taken together and purchased by a quality manufacturer. Dr. Jason Theodosakis is an expert on arthritis ("The Arthritis Cure") and offers many suggestions for alleviating symptoms of arthritis on his website: www.drtheo.com.

- **Constipation:** As we age, our digestive tract slows down which often leads to chronic constipation. As with other conditions, a healthy diet is imperative. Whole fruits and vegetables provide the necessary fiber to keep the bowels moving. Staying well-hydrated keeps the stool soft and pliable so as to move through the colon. If your loved one is not evacuating at least daily, some natural foods and herbs can help move the bowels. In addition to flax seed oil and water, mild laxatives in tea form are available and can be purchased at most grocery or health stores. My favorite is "Smooth Move" tea by Traditional Medicinals. Specific foods that help move the bowels are dried plums (prunes), red beets (steamed), and apples, which can be peeled and pureed into a fresh, unsweetened apple sauce.

- **Anxiety/Worry:** Anxiety is normal for aging adults as they begin to lose control over their lives. For some, it's financial, such as worry over the ability to pay their bills. There are many resources available to assist with financial management, and many are listed in this resource guide. Support of family and friends can alleviate day to day concerns, such as picking up the mail, grocery shopping, and hiring lawn and other home improvement services. Even if there is no expressed reason for anxiety, just talking can help your loved one feel relief. Of course, excessive worry or anxiety that impedes quality of life, such as poor sleep or loss of appetite, may require medical intervention to rule out underlying disease.

- **Failing Eyesight:** Failing eyesight is common as we age, and cataracts, glaucoma, and macular degeneration in particular are a growing concern. As with many other diseases, inflammation is the main reason our eyesight fails us, so reversing this process can help slow or stop retinal damage. Antioxidant foods and supplements that are rich in Vitamin C and Vitamin A are helpful. Examples are citrus fruits, melons, strawberries, blueberries, carrots, squash, and yams. An annual eye exam is always indicated for the elderly.

- **Hearing Loss:** Hearing loss is an insidious problem that usually develops over many years. It is important to recognize hearing loss as a potential problem, as often times other age-related problems are diagnosed without recognizing that hearing loss is the actual root of the problem. For example, an aging adult who exhibits symptoms of depression, forgetfulness, or social isolation may actually be introverting as a result of not being able to engage with the world around them due to hearing loss. Make sure that your loved one gets a hearing test each year, and a proper-fitting hearing aid if needed. You may be surprised at the change you see!

- **Senile Dementia:** Forgetfulness, disorientation, slow reflexes, and social isolation are some of the signs of dementia. While minor forgetfulness may be expected, dementia that disrupts the quality of one's life should be addressed. Visual reminders, such as a large calendar for writing appointments and important dates are helpful, as are telephones with large numbers. Medications that are separated and labeled by day and time will help to remind seniors of important daily doses. Be sure to watch for signs that dementia may be creating safety issues for your loved one. Some examples may be chronic, unkempt appearance and poor hygiene; forgetting to turn off the stove burners after cooking; going to check the mail and becoming disoriented and forgetting why they left the house or where home is. If your loved one lives alone, make sure that when you visit you observe for subtle signs of forgetfulness, such as medications still in Tuesday's container when it's Friday, or familiar items being out of place.

- **Osteoporosis:** Most common to women, osteoporosis (bone loss) is one of the major reasons for fractured hips. Bone loss can be prevented with a proper diet rich in calcium, as well as by eliminating acid forming foods, such as caffeinated beverages and meat products. Eating a calcium rich diet with plenty of dark green vegetables will keep the system less acidic, a condition which creates the loss of calcium in bones. Vitamin D is needed in order for the body to utilize calcium, so supplementation is important. Supplements that also provide magnesium (the "anti-stress" mineral) will help the body better utilize calcium.

- **Pain:** Try to find the source of the pain. If it is structural (bones/muscles), a chiropractic consultation may help. Stomach pain may indicate poor digestion, requiring extra nutrients, such as probiotics or digestive enzymes. Lower abdominal pain may be constipation. Back pain may be from poor posture or inactivity, such as sitting for long periods. It may also be from a worn-out bed mattress. Bladder pain may indicate a urinary tract infection. Head pain may be structural, such as a pinched neck nerve or circulatory congestion, or signs of a more serious condition such as high blood pressure or stroke. If you can determine the most practical reason for the pain, try natural remedies for relief. Anti-inflammatory herbs and supplements may be helpful, such as ginger or turmeric (curry) and flax seed oil. If no relief is obtained from natural interventions within a reasonable amount of time, a medical consultation may be indicated.

- **Urinary Tract Infections (UTI):** Dehydration is a major reason for many ailments that the elderly suffer, including forgetfulness, aches, pains, and urinary tract infections. Make sure your parent knows to drink water. Bladder muscles relax with age and sensation in the bladder may be lost. Have your loved one get in the habit of emptying their bladder every three to four hours, even when there is no urgency to go. Retaining urine for long periods creates a distended bladder which, over time, diminishes sensitivity and creates an environment for bacteria to grow. Cranberries are a natural bladder antiseptic and cranberry capsules work well to help prevent bladder infection. Cranberry juices are not recommended, as they contain a lot of sugar, which may contribute to the problem. Cranberry capsules, on the other hand, are concentrated cranberries without sugar. If your loved one has difficulty swallowing capsules, unsweetened cranberry tea is available. You can also open capsules and sprinkle the ingredients over food. If signs of bladder infection are present, such as burning and foul-smelling urine, make sure that your loved one drinks lots of unsweetened fluids. If fever is present, consult with your parent's physician for appropriate medical care.

Conclusion

While we can't beat Mother Nature in fighting the aging process, we certainly can slow it down. By being mindful of healthful living and using naturopathic modalities, you can make a difference in the life of your aging loved one by helping them to make natural and healthy choices that will improve their well-being and quality of life.

References

Weil, Andrew, M.D., (1998) *Natural Health, Natural Medicine,* N.Y., Houghton Mifflin Company.

Cheraskin, M.D., D.M.D., (1999) *Human Health and Homeostasis,* Al: Clayton College Natural Reader Press.

Mitchell, Stewart, (2001) *A Practical Guide to Naturopathy,*

OH: Custom Publishing.

Willet, Walter, M.D., (2001) *Eat, Drink and be Healthy*, N.Y.: Free Press–a division of Simon & Shuster, Inc.

Lindlahr, Henry, M.D., (2005) *Philosophy of Natural Therapeutics*, U.K.: Random House.

Theodasakis, Jason, M.D., (2004) *The Arthritis Cure,* N.Y.: St. Martin's Griffin.

Blaylock, Russell, M.D., (1997) *Excitotoxins– The Taste that Kills,* N.M.: Health Press NA, Inc.

Ottoboni, Alice, Ph.D. and Ottoboni, Fred, M.P.H., Ph.D. ((2002) *The Modern Nutritional Diseases,* NN: Vincente Books, Inc.

Office on Aging: http://www.hhs.gov/aging/index.html

United States Department of Agriculture.

http://www.mypyramid.gov

Nature's Sunshine Products–Manufacturer of whole food and herbal supplements. Products can be ordered online at my website: http://KrisWoodsRN.mynsp.com/

National Strategies for Suicide Prevention, *Department of Health and Human Services*, USA. http://mentalhealth.samhsa.gov/suicideprevention/elderly.asp

Pollan, Michael. (2009) *Food Rules,* N.Y.: Penguin Press.

Eat Right–Academy of Nutrition and Dietetics. "Healthy Eating for Older Adults". https://www.eatright.org/food/nutrition/dietary-guidelines-and-myplate/healthy-eating-for-older-adults

Kris Woods has been educating patients on holistic health practices as a Registered Nurse for more than 40 years. She began studying herbal medicine in 1999, and earned an advanced degree in Naturopathy in 2010. As a health educator, she guides clients to wellness by implementing the principles of holistic healing and self-care for disease management. Kris resides in Camarillo, California.

Notes

Notes

21

The Diagnosis and Management of Vascular Disease in the Elderly

ଔ

JASON CHIRIANO
DO FACS RPVI Board Certified Vascular Surgeon

The population in the United States continues to live longer, and those born in the baby boomer generation are now approaching an age where they face a significant risk for developing vascular disease. Cardiovascular disease includes blockages in the blood vessels that supply the heart, brain, intestines, and extremities. These blockages are due to a buildup of cholesterol, fatty deposits, and calcium in the walls of the blood vessels. Once this happens, individuals are at significantly higher risk of experiencing heart attacks, strokes, and limb loss. The other category of vascular disease that occurs includes aneurysmal disease. An aneurysm is a weakening of the wall of the blood vessels which causes them to dilate. This can happen in any vessel but commonly occurs in the aorta. The aorta is the largest blood vessel in the body and runs from the heart down through the abdomen. Aneurysms can rupture, leading to death from hemorrhage. This chapter will focus on identifying and managing the risk factors that lead to the development of aneurysmal disease, peripheral vascular disease, and cerebrovascular disease. Additionally, the current screening guidelines for diagnosing this disease process will be discussed.

Risk Factors

The risk factors for developing vascular disease include, but are not limited to, tobacco use, high cholesterol, diabetes, male gender, and increasing age.

Tobacco use leads to an annual excess mortality in the US of 350,000 deaths. This is roughly equal to the entire US casualties incurred during World War II. Further, it also leads to a direct increase in health care costs of $16 billion and indirect costs of $37 billion. Despite these statistics, those that are addicted to smoking and nicotine continue their behavior. Statistics show that it takes at least nine attempts on average to succeed in smoking cessation in the long-term. During this time, those that continue to smoke will continue to develop and progress in their vascular disease. They have almost four times the risk of developing significant vascular disease compared to those who are tobacco free.

The current diet in the US lends itself to the development of hypercholesteremia (high cholesterol) as well as diabetes. It is common for Americans to eat on-the-go, and the current environment supplies an endless feast of inexpensive food on every corner. Fast food diets include highly fatty foods, with high cholesterol content. The typical American diet is also fairly low in fruits and vegetables and the fiber they offer. Further, obesity is on the rise and is now a full-blown epidemic, which also leads to an increased risk of developing diabetes as well as high cholesterol. Those with diabetes and/or high cholesterol have nearly a three times increased risk of developing significant vascular disease compared to those without diabetes or high cholesterol.

Management of Noncoronary Vascular Disease in the Elderly

Management of Hypercholesteremia

The best intervention for hypercholesteremia (high cholesterol) is prevention. However, when talking about patients with advanced age, prevention is not the aim. The focus should be on lifestyle modification and pharmacologic therapy that will help to lower the cholesterol to acceptable levels that will help prevent cardiovascular complications including heart attack and stroke. The current American Heart Association Guidelines state that high intensity statin therapy should be used to lower low density lipoprotein levels (LDL-C) by 50%. Statin drugs are very potent in lowering cholesterol, but can have side effects of liver problems, muscle cramping, and rhabdomyolysis (a break down in muscle). Sometimes patients cannot tolerate this class of medications due to these side effects, and caretakers of patients that take these should be aware of this. If patients develop these side effects, their primary care physician should be notified immediately.

Abdominal Aortic Aneurysm

The prevalence of abdominal aortic aneurysm (AAA) is 5 times more common in men than women. The incidence increases from 1.3% in men and 0% of women aged 45-54 years, up to 12.5% in men and 5.2% of women aged 75-84 years. The U.S. Preventive Services Task Force recommends screening with abdominal ultrasonography in all men aged 65-75 years old who have ever smoked and selectively in men who have never smoked. The recommendations in women are less clear, but women who have smoked and are over age 65 should probably be screened as well. Additionally, anyone who has a first-degree relative with an AAA, and any history of cardiovascular disease, high cholesterol, or high blood pressure should also be screened. The purpose of screening this patient population is to aid in early detection and eventual repair prior to rupture. Aneurysms that are over 5-5.5cm in diameter or that have more than 0.5cm growth in 6 months should be electively repaired. Ruptured aneurysms carry a 50% mortality at home. Additionally, 50% of patients that make it to the hospital will eventually expire even with repair. This is in contrast to elective repair that now can be done with minimal invasion and carries less than a 1% mortality.

Peripheral Arterial Disease

The incidence of peripheral arterial disease (PAD) rises significantly with age. Nearly 25% of adults under 80 years of age will have some evidence of peripheral vascular disease. This includes the process in which the vessels of the legs and sometimes the arms become blocked with cholesterol and calcium. This is a disease known as atherosclerosis. Once the vessels become blocked, individuals are at increased risk of having pain in the limbs with exertion. This is due to the fact that the muscles cannot get enough oxygen when they are being used, which of course leads to decreased activity and a more sedentary life style, which then leads to more heart disease and earlier mortality. Additionally, PAD increases the risk of limb loss due to non-healing wounds and gangrene. Once individuals lose a limb, they will have a significantly decreased quality of life, decreased independence, and earlier mortality.

Most patients with this disease will be asymptomatic (90%), meaning they will not have any leg pain, no history of stroke, or any wounds. However, it is important to look for this disease process in older adults as it is an independent marker for systemic cardiovascular events such as heart attack and stroke. Patients who have the formerly mentioned risk factors should talk to their doctors about being screened for peripheral vascular disease. This is usually a simple process and involves a thorough history and physical exam.

It is important to diagnose this disease process in the elderly, as there are many treatments that can help prevent death and disability. Lifestyle changes are of utmost importance. Adherence to a Mediterranean diet high in lean protein, fruits, and vegetables has been independently associated with decreased mortality. Additionally, daily exercise and smoking cessation are also associated with improved life spans and halting of the progression of peripheral vascular disease. The medical management of patients with PAD includes antiplatelet therapy (Aspirin 81mg every day), and statin therapy (Lipitor, Zocor, etc.). Together, these have helped to both decrease the incidence of heart attacks and strokes and lower cholesterol. Patients that have severe limb symptoms will need procedures performed that bring more blood flow to the legs. A multimodal, comprehensive treatment program in elderly patients will benefit them by allowing for improved quality of life, decreased complications of cardiovascular disease, and longer life spans.

Cerebral Vascular Disease

The risk of suffering a major stroke goes up significantly when there is a blockage of the carotid arteries that supply the brain. Blockages in the carotid arteries can be diagnosed via an ultrasound of these vessels. There is no current recommendation for routine screening of asymptomatic individuals with this modality. However, it should be considered as a source of subclinical infarcts in the elderly that has been shown to lead to an increased incidence of dementia (multi-infarct dementia). Additionally, screening should be obtained in any patient that has had a transient ischemic attack (TIA). Individuals can have transient weakness in one side of the body, speech difficulties, facial droop, or acute blindness in one eye. These attacks can last from minutes to hours and usually resolve, but they can be a warning of a coming major stroke. Strokes are the nations 3rd leading cause of disability in the US and result in a significant decreased quality of life for the patient, a significant increase in burden to the family members of the patient, and a large increase in the use of health care expenditures to care for these patients. The treatment of carotid artery blockage involves medical management which includes aspiring and/or Plavix to help keep the blood from clotting. The surgical management includes a carotid endarterectomy which is a way to clean out the artery, as well as, carotid stenting. Carotid stenting is a minimally invasive treatment during which a metal cage is deployed in the carotid under X-ray. Patients usually tolerate these procedures well with minimal complications and are usually discharged from the hospital in one to two days. Carotid disease is only one cause of stroke, but it is treatable, preventing a later debilitating event. Early detection will lead to early treatment and improved long-term outcomes in these patients.

Natural Remedies to Improve Cardiovascular Health in the Elderly Patient

A lot of aging patients have poor access to health care, or are on several medications that require multiple prescriptions and trips to the pharmacy. There are several natural remedies that can be purchased at your local stores that do not require prescriptions. Additionally, they can be purchased online. Below is a list of these medications:

- Garlic: This can be found in a variety of foods, but can also be bought in pill form. It has been used for hundreds of years due to its ability to boost heart health. It is thought that it keeps arteries flexible. Further, it helps to lower cholesterol, blood pressure, and inflammation

- Coenzyme Q-10: This is an antioxidant and also helps cells make energy. Additionally, it may mitigate some of the side effects of the statin drugs mentioned above.

- Red Yeast Rice: This is a fermented mix of rice and yeast. This helps to reduce cholesterol naturally and has a statin like effect.

- Flaxseed: This natural remedy is high in omega 3 fatty acids, which is beneficial for overall heart health. It is also thought to help reduce cholesterol as well. The seed should be ground and milled; otherwise, it will just pass through the body without being absorbed.

- Turmeric: This is one of nature's most powerful antioxidants/anti-inflammatory. The inflammatory state is thought to be a culprit for many ailments. When the body is in a constant state of inflammation, the immune system does not work as well, the stress hormones are higher, and overall health is affected. By reducing the amount of overall inflammation in the body, it can heal naturally and a better state of health can be achieved.

The aging population poses several challenges to the health care system as well as the family members that are involved in their care. The care of these patients must be multidisciplinary and include strategies that help to prevent the development of chronic diseases and manage currently existing conditions. The above recommendations serve as a general guide to help the caregivers of these patients navigate the complicated maze of the health care system as it currently exists. This should serve as one piece in the puzzle to help elderly patients live longer and healthier lives.

Resources:

Cholesterol Management Guide–www.heart.org/cholesterol

Peripheral Artery Disease (PAD) Resources–www.heart.org/en/health-topics/peripheral-artery-disease/pad-resources

Aneurysm screening recommendations–www.uspreventiveservicestaskforce.org

Kernan W, Ovbiagele B, Black H etal. Guidelines for the prevention of stroke in patients with stroke and transient ischemic attack. Stroke 2014; 45: 2160-2236.

REGEN HEALING CENTERS

"Offering state of the art comprehensive care to all patients that suffer from chronic disease"

We employ a multidisciplinary approach to chronic disease and employ the following healing modalities

1. Stem cell therapy–quality stem cells from the only FDA approved lab in the United States, harvested from umbilical cord blood

2. Light and magnetic therapy

3. Nutritional consultation

4. Complete medical management of chronic disease

Contact our center to lead to happier healthier life:

951-235-1181

Notes

22

How Can a Geriatric Care Manager Help?

ುಞ

CAROLYN MICHAELIS
RN, BSN, MPA
Certified Care Manager

An Aging Life Care Professional, also known as a Geriatric Care Manager, is a health and human services specialist who acts as a guide and <u>advocate</u> for families who are caring for older relatives or disabled adults, or for the older adult themselves. She/He is educated and experienced in any of several fields related to Aging Life Care/care management, including, but not limited to counseling, gerontology, mental health, nursing, occupational therapy, physical therapy, psychology, or social work, with a specialized focus on issues related to aging and elder care. Many of them have additional education or training in dementia, legal issues, insurance, finances, family mediation, and other fields which assist families and adults in making wise decisions regarding care.

What Can a Geriatric Care Manager Do for You?

Aging Life Care™, also known as geriatric care management, is a holistic, client-centered approach to caring for older adults or others facing ongoing health challenges. Aging Life Care Professionals provide the answers at a time of uncertainty. Their guidance leads families to the actions and decisions that ensure quality care and an optimal life for those they love, thus reducing worry, stress, and time off of work for family caregivers.

Aging Life Care Professionals can serve the needs of their clients by providing:

- a comprehensive assessment and preparation of a care plan tailored for each individual's circumstances (The plan may be modified, in consultation with client and family, as circumstances change.)

- identification and engagement of local, cost-effective resources as needed

- personalized and caring service, focused on the individual's wants and needs

- accessibility, typically available 24 hours a day, 7 days a week
- continuity of care maintained through communications coordinated among doctors and other professionals and service providers to resolve or prevent conflicting information
- family communication, such as reports sent to multiple family members
- cost containment (Inappropriate placements, duplication of services, and unnecessary hospitalizations are avoided by planning and management.)
- quality control (All Aging Life Care professional members follow ALCA's Standards of Practice and Code of Ethics. See website for description.)

Aging Life Care Professionals Have Expertise in 8 Knowledge Areas

Health and Disability. From physical to mental health and dementia-related problems, Aging Life Care Professionals™ interact with the health care system effectively and frequently. ALC Professionals attend doctor appointments and facilitate communication between doctor, client, and family. These professionals help determine types of services–including home health and hospice–that are right for a client and assist in engaging and monitoring those services.

Financial. Services may include consulting with a client's accountant or Power of Attorney. ALC Professionals provide information on Federal and state entitlements, connecting families to local programs when appropriate. They also help clients and families with insurance concerns, claims, and applications.

Housing. ALC Professionals help families and clients evaluate and select the appropriate level of housing or residential options.

Families. ALC Professionals help families adjust, cope, and problem-solve around long-distance and in-home caregiving–addressing care concerns, internal conflicts, and differences of opinion about long-term care planning.

Local Resources. ALC Professionals know the local resources in their communities and know how services are accessed.

Advocacy. ALC Professionals are strong and effective advocates for clients and their families, promoting the client's wishes with health care and other providers.

Legal. ALC Professionals refer to legal experts, like elder law attorneys, estate planners, and Powers of Attorney. Some ALC Professionals provide expert opinion for courts in determining level of care and establishing client needs.

Crisis Intervention. ALC Professionals offer crisis intervention when it is needed, helping clients navigate through emergency departments, hospitalizations, and rehabilitation stays and ensuring that adequate care is available to the client. For families that live at a distance, this can be a much-needed 24/7 emergency contact.

What are the Signs We Might Need an ALCP/GMC?

Do you suspect your loved one needs help? Each case is different and there are many signs that indicate it's time for outside help.

Here are a few:

- Declining health (weight loss, fatigue, depression, etc.)
- Home maintenance neglect
- Stacks of unpaid bills or mail
- Refusing to go to the doctor or missing scheduled appointments
- Frequent ER visits or hospitalizations
- Not taking medications properly
- Noticeable decrease in maintaining hygiene
- Difficulty driving
- Excessive spending
- Trouble addressing issues in the medical care system

- Needs to determine whether to stay at home or move to a facility

- Is confused about financial or legal situation

- Does not have family support or it is inadequate due to distance or other factors such as there is disagreement in the family regarding care needs and plans

If you see one or more of these signs, an ALC Professional (Geriatric Care Manager) would be a great solution for you and your family!

So, where do you find one?

How to Select an ALC Professional (Geriatric Care Manager)

Fortunately, the Aging Life Care Association makes it easy to find a qualified professional care manager. Access the website at www.aginglifecare.org and you will find the tab "Find a Care Manager." That will bring you to a page that will allow you to enter a zip code or a city and select how far to search: 25 miles, 50 miles, etc. In some rural areas, you may need to enter 50 miles to obtain names of professionals who service that area.

All members of the ALCA™ have pledged to adhere to a code of ethics and practice norms. The persons listed will have their credentials on the listing, so you can identify whether you think that a social worker background would fit your needs best; or if there are multiple medical issues, perhaps you would want to select a care manager with a nursing background. Keep in mind that many times RNs have Social Workers working for them and vice versa. ALCA™ members do not accept "referral fees" from resources to which they refer, as this creates a conflict of interest.

They function as the advocate of the person they serve, not of facilities or providers.

Next, call the agency you have selected and interview with them. ALCA™ members are very willing to talk to you and hear your situation and provide you with a synopsis of what they can do for you. During this interview, you can determine if you feel you can work with this person well. If possible, call more than one company for comparison.

How Much Will Services Cost? Does Insurance Cover Costs?

Aging Life Professionals work for you and your family. Costs will vary based on expertise and location. Most companies charge by the time spent on services for your family.

Health insurance will not pay for Professional Care Managers, however there are some Long-Term Care insurance policies that cover Care Management, so check your policies for definition. Also check with your employer's EAP programs, as many are now providing care management consultation in order to decrease the loss of productivity of their staff who are trying to balance caring for aging parents with doing their jobs!

Additional Support

Aging Life Care Association www.aginglifecare.org

National Academy of Certified Care Managers www.naccm.net

Commission for Case Manager Certification www.ccmcertification.org

National Association of Social Workers www.socialworkers.org

Alzheimer's Association www.alz.org

Notes

_____

_____

_____

_____

_____

_____

_____

_____

_____

_____

_____

_____

_____

_____

_____

_____

_____

_____

Notes

23

Caregiving from a Distance

Cℬ

KAREN GRIFFITH
Geriatric Care Manager

Just because you don't live close enough to oversee daily activities for your loved one, or you're not able to respond in case of an emergency, doesn't mean you can't be involved in the caregiving of your loved one. You can be a valuable part of the caregiving team by becoming the information gatherer or the coordinator of services. This chapter is meant to help you find your way on the journey of caregiving from a distance. It is not always easy, but it can be made easier if you take it one step at a time.

Understand the Situation

Spend some time trying to understand the situation. Talk with your parent, your siblings, your parent's friends and the people who interact with them most to find out what their most pressing needs are. Ask them to share all of the information they can about their present situation and hopes for the future, and what they see as possible solutions to the challenges they're facing. What needs to be done? What are the options? What will work best? In addition to speaking with all involved parties, you will want to acquire important documents and pay attention to legal and financial details.

Basic Information: Complete and accurate information is essential for long-distance caregiving. You must have accurate information about your parent's personal, health, financial, and legal records. This can be challenging because parents are sometimes reluctant to share really personal items with their children. You will need to reassure them that this information may be needed in an emergency and they may not be able to help you then. The following is a handy list of basic information you need to have available so you are prepared to be an advocate for your loved one:

- Full legal name and residence
- Birth date and place

- Social security number
- Employer(s) and dates of employment
- Education and military records
- Sources of income and assets; investment income (stocks, bonds, property)
- Insurance policies, bank accounts, deeds, investments, and other valuables
- Most recent income tax returns
- Money owed, to whom and when payments are due
- Credit card and charge account names and numbers

Important Documentation: In your search for vital information, you may discover that your parent does not have their legal affairs in order. They need a current will, estate plan, health care power of attorney, financial power of attorney and HIPPA authorization (Health Insurance Portability and Accountability Act). It is essential that all of those documents are in place and current. If the parent becomes so ill they cannot make decisions or express their wishes, you are then able to make choices for them. A certified Elder Law Attorney can prepare these documents.

It is important that your parent appoints a *financial power of attorney* so their bills will be paid if they are no longer capable of doing it themselves. The financial power of attorney will enable you to access retirement accounts, pension plans and banking accounts. If the power of attorney is properly worded, it can also allow you to do real estate transactions. Without a financial power of attorney, it will be necessary to get a conservatorship through the courts. This is a costly process and takes several months to get in place.

The *HIPPA authorization* allows a person to designate who may have access to their personal health and medical records in the event that they cannot make this authorization because of injury or other incapacity. So you, as a long-distance caregiver, will need to be named in a HIPPA to be able to speak with doctors, hospitals or rehabilitation/skilled nursing facilities about status or treatment.

The *health care power of attorney* will allow you to make decisions about treatments should your parent be unable to do so. It is supremely important that you discuss what their wishes are about tube feeding, ventilators and dialysis. Find out if they want CPR or other heroic measures. Try to be very specific as to what they want done in a variety of situations. Then make sure these wishes are recorded in the medical record and available to any caregiver in the home, nursing home or hospital. There are several states that require a POLST form. That means Physician Orders for Life-Sustaining Treatment. Beginning in 2009, this form is used in California to clarify whether a patient would want CPR if they were found with no pulse and not breathing. It also gives choices about medical intervention if they have a pulse and are breathing (e.g. comfort measures only; limited intervention such as antibiotics, IV's or full treatment- intubation, advanced airway intervention and a transfer to hospital if indicated). It is important that you know what your family member desires in regards to these treatments so there is no confusion should use of this form be required. Often end of life care is more about quality of life care– reducing symptoms and pain management. You and your family need to consult with health care professionals about the impact of giving or withholding treatments.

Formulate a Plan
Once you have some possible solutions in mind, prioritize them and then gather information about the costs of each solution. For

example, if in-home assistance is needed, who can provide this help and how much will it cost? Perhaps some home modifications are needed–you can contact contractors, get bids, and coordinate their services even if you are not in the area.

Financial Preparation–Caregiving requires a lot of time and money. In-home care, assisted living, and skilled nursing costs can quickly exhaust savings accounts and other assets. You really need a good plan to prepare for these expenses. You may need to confer with an elder law attorney or a reputable financial planner to help formulate a viable plan to cover possible caregiving costs.

Organize a Team

Because of the distance, you are going to need a team of people to support you in this effort, but you can be the one who organizes and coordinates them according to their roles and the value they bring to the caregiving process. You will need the names, contact information, and support of doctors, care providers, transportation organizers, bill payers, companions, attorneys, financial advisors, and religious leaders. The members of your team should be able to provide the services and care to your loved one so they are safe and comfortable. It is important to communicate with all the members of your team by telephone or email on a pre- arranged schedule.

Remind yourself that the team is responsible for the caregiving–not any one person. As the team coordinator, your primary job is to hold each member of the team accountable for their tasks. If they fail to do what they've committed to do, then it will be your responsibility to find a replacement. Be willing to modify your team or your caregiving plan if and when a situation changes.

Communicate Constructively

Clear and constructive communication goes a long way in building an effective caregiving team. Make sure that everyone understands their roles, and that they need to report to you regularly regarding that role in your parent's care.

Do What You Can

What are your strengths and how can they best be used on your caregiving team? Be realistic. If you aren't good with numbers and paying bills, then that responsibility is best left to someone who loves to do it. Trying to cover areas of care that cause you stress will defeat the team approach. Ideally each member of your team will be able to take on what is easiest and most rewarding for them.

When the time comes for children to provide help for aging parents, many things need to be in place, and children who live at a distance have overwhelming challenges if unprepared.

Caregiving Support

If you live at a distance and simply don't have the time and energy to oversee the caregiving responsibilities, there is another option. Geriatric Care Managers are usually Social Workers or Nurses who have experience working with older people. They are very skilled in doing assessments which is a comprehensive report on the situation and recommendations for what assistance, home modifications or services are needed. They can also locate and coordinate services, oversee care, assist with paperwork and provide counseling. They are like a "professional relative" to help you with long-distance caregiving. The Aging Life Care Association can help you find one in your area. Their website is www.aginglifecare.org.

Take Care of Yourself

Caregiving, whether in your home, across town, or at a distance is an extra responsibility which can be exhausting and stressful. You need to take care of yourself and always be prepared with back-up options. If you have a "Plan B" in mind, then it will be less stressful if something doesn't work out. Here are some quick tips to make your caregiving experience easier:

Expect changes – they _will_ happen.
Share your story – sharing does magically lighten the load.
Find a caregiver support group and participate.
If you can't find one, start one.
Remember to always _take care of you first_.

KAREN GRIFFITH

After having worked with the disabled community for over 18 years, Karen Griffith recently joined our law firm as our Geriatric Care Coordinator. Karen has her Bachelor's Degree in Social Work from the University of Nebraska. She is a member of the National Association of Professional Geriatric Care Managers as well as its Western Region chapter. Karen is also licensed as a Notary Public in California.

Karen specializes in working with seniors and the disabled. She is available to assist clients with the selection of an appropriate nursing home or assisted care facility. Where the disabled person or senior desires to remain in their home, Karen is available to assess what modifications will be necessary to allow the senior or disabled person to have the greatest amount of freedom and accessibility. Where the client is in a nursing home or assisted living facility, Karen is available to attend and actively advocate for the needs of a client in patient care meetings.

Karen serves on the Steering Committee for the Inland Empire Palliative Care Coalition and on its Education Committee. Karen is active with many support groups for patients and families of patients with senile dementia or Alzheimer's Disease, Parkinson's Disease, Lou Gehrig's Disease, Muscular Sclerosis, stroke and other debilitating diseases.

Karen resides in Riverside, California. She has 2 children and 1 granddaughter. Her hobbies include gardening (she is a Master Composter), singing, antiques and collectables, cooking, and going to yard sales.

Notes

_____

_____

_____

_____

_____

_____

_____

_____

_____

_____

_____

_____

_____

_____

_____

_____

_____

Notes

_____

_____

_____

_____

_____

_____

_____

_____

_____

_____

_____

_____

_____

_____

_____

_____

_____

24

Conflict Resolution: Creative Solutions for Tough Times

ᘒ

DANIELA BUMANN
CEO Vibrant Living International

> *"The most motivating thing one person can do for another is to listen." – Roy Moody*

As a caregiver, you may come across challenges that require you to learn more about solving conflict with style. In this chapter, you will find a road map to help you develop the most important qualities, virtues, and communication skills you need. You will learn what your personality/communication style is, and how to easily recognize others' styles as well. This will serve as a guide to help you create better relationships and support you through the challenges you may face as a caregiver. Most importantly, it will teach you how to more effectively collaborate with your family, and to create win-win solutions in order to get on the same page and ensure that your loved one does not have to deal with family conflict in addition to the challenges they are already facing.

Since I can remember, I have been passionate about recognizing, on a personal level and then coaching others in my professional life, how to demonstrate and cultivate the attitude, tools, and virtues that foster collaboration, vision, and inspiration.

Some of the virtues or qualities that cultivate this enhanced character development are:

Mindfulness–paying attention to the cues within and around you

- *Tolerance* of others uniqueness (diversity)
- *Respect* and *Understanding*
- *Compassion* (for self and others)
- *Willingness to Listen* in order to understand
- *Ability to NOT Take Things Personally*

These virtues can open the pathway to amazing collaborations and get almost any group of people on the same page. When driven by the absolute desire to simply "see the best" and most positive potential in everyone (whether they demonstrated their best side, or have their counterpart, as in Jackal and Hyde, over as a guest), these traits will bring people together for the common good of taking care of their loved one.

Most interestingly, when you set the intention to embody these virtues, you very often just by simply holding that clear vision and focus, can bring about those traits in others, even if they are irate. This can then enable you to support and help them in demonstrating their best behavior, just as you did yours. By just "not taking it personally" and by not reacting to what they possibly conceived as an attack to their ego or well-being, you can get good results. That's it. If you both react, you will both be stuck in the tangle, and the drama and play of "power games" will have just begun.

I have seen many people choose to stay in that drama all their lives, but I have seen others make a conscious choice to grow and learn more about themselves and others in order to break the old pattern. They have chosen to go against their behavioral conditioning, which at times seems to almost have a "seductive" lure to continue on the same route. Instead of giving in to the desire to fight, blame, manipulate, be right, and even control others, they have chosen to be in command of their own lives.

In my coaching work, it's always been exciting to see someone recognize and understand from their heart that they cannot 'grow' their partner, loved one, co-worker, or sibling by blaming and attacking them. Even though there may be legitimate hurt, reacting just keeps us stuck in a victim role, creating more of the same drama. Accepting responsibility for our own behavior, and accepting that we are all different, frees us from the merry-go-round. It will liberate you to create more empowered relationships and support you in becoming a better caregiver, while helping you navigate through the challenges of being a loved one advocate.

Caregiving Statistics

Right now, more than 50 million people provide care for a chronically ill, disabled, or aged family member or friend during any given year.

- 51% of caregivers get sick or die before the person they are caring for.

- Approximately 60% of family caregivers are women.

- 30% of family caregivers caring for seniors are themselves age 65 or over, and another 15% are between 45 and 54 years of age.

A Unique Mix of Challenges

As a caregiver or loved one advocate, you face a complex and unique set of challenges that can bring up unresolved emotions. Emotions from your childhood as well as current feelings of fear, worry, and guilt of placing your loved one, together with your own unique circumstances, can lead to overwhelm and conflict with other family members. Generally, one person tends to be very involved with the care of your loved one, while others do not want to assume or share responsibility, or may even choose to stay in denial over the circumstances. Remember, the aging process your loved one is experiencing is normal. It's not your fault (you have done nothing wrong), nor is it your responsibility. How you *respond* is your responsibility, and choosing to *be* loving and demonstrate objective thinking and compassion can make this a "healing time" on many fronts.

This overwhelming time can bring out the best and worst in others. Remember to be gentle with yourself, get the help you need, and know that everybody is doing the best they can. The key is to find a "common" ground and to create a solution that serves your loved one's needs.

Got Conflict? Fact or Fiction

Fiction: *Conflict is a normal part of daily communication.*

Fact: *While some conflict is healthy and can have positive results, most conflict can be avoided by improving one's listening and communication skills.*

The good news is that there is lots you CAN do about it!

Don't Take It Personally

Even though this can be a tumultuous time in bringing all the family dynamics back into the mix, please remember that it is NOT about you. This is not the time to hold onto grudges and bring up old conflicts and hurts. It's time to focus on the common denominator, which is to be your loved one's advocate. Depersonalizing your feelings from the current situation is most essential in order to find the best solution to fit your loved one's needs.

Speak From the Heart

Whether you are the main caregiver or one that has thus far been more peripherally involved in your loved one's care, the words you choose can create a bridge to understanding, or bring added pressure and confusion to the process. Speak from the heart. This is not the time to be judgmental, engage in labeling or criticizing one another. It is time for all to extend themselves–to learn and apply more tools to better understand themselves and others. Most importantly, use care and sensitivity in addressing the issues around your family members and especially your loved one. If you have to, *agree to disagree* in order to get on the same page for the greater good.

Seek First to Understand, Then to Be Understood
(Stephen R. Covey)
It's human nature that we all want to be understood. "You just don't understand me!" is something we may have all yelled or at least thought to ourselves at one point or another. The key here is that often there can be a lot of words going back and forth, without much communication going on at all. We are all different people with different needs, and the more you learn about the other's needs, how to treat them, and how to communicate with their behavioral or personality style, the more effortless your communication will become. This is an essential key to the success of your partnership as loved one advocates.

Find a Solution Together
First and foremost, get very clear on your goal, focus, and intention in the process of working together to create a solution. Practice your listening skills. Please use empathy. And do not shoot the messenger. It's not about being right or wrong, good or bad, but for all of you to set your differences aside for your loved one's greatest sake. Nurturing each other along will be much more productive than criticizing one another at every opportunity. Even though you may be upset with a family member and/or the situation at hand, you can use the following *affirmation tool* in order to help you shift into a more positive and loving perspective.

Key to Success
Schedule family conversations frequently.
Don't try to solve every problem in one meeting.

Peace Centering Exercise

First, set the stage by closing your eyes, relaxing your mind, and/ or engaging in prayer. Get very present and breathe deeply into your body. When you are ready, repeat the following affirmation *with feeling* out loud (or your adapted version) 3 times, paying particular attention to how you feel afterwards. You may use this before a family meeting or several times a day for peace of mind. It's simple, but very effective.

> Even though I'm feeling _____ and I'm also upset about _____, I'm *now* choosing to let go of all anger, fear, and resentment. I am *now* choosing to see the goodness within myself and each member of my family. I am *now* allowing for a harmonious solution to occur–filled with peace, clarity, understanding, and well-being for all.

Understand and Interact Appropriately with Behavioral Styles

(The DiSC® Behavioral System)

Below you will learn more about your own personality and behavioral style, and how to recognize others' behavioral styles in order to defuse challenges, solve conflict, and improve your communication skills. I have found my work with the DiSC Behavioral System and Personalized Assessments to be very eye-opening and a very powerful tool for conflict prevention.

The success of personal and professional relationships lies in understanding yourself and others, while realizing the impact of personal behavior on others. For nearly thirty years, more than 30 million people have unlocked their potential to productive communication and relationships through the DiSC® Behavioral learning approach.

Using the DiSC® Behavioral System allows one to use nonjudgmental language in order to explore and shift behavioral habits that are not productive, and are not conducive to creating powerful communications and relationships.

Self-Assessment: Identify Your Personality Type & Communication Style

Please put check marks by the traits that best describe you on the following pages. Try to check only the traits that *really* describe you, NOT the ones that you'd like to be described by. Remember! This is not a test. There is no right or wrong answer.

– Fast Paced/Task Oriented –

The Dominance (D) Behavioral Dimension

Check all that apply to you.

__ aggressive	__ dictatorial	__ outspoken
__ ambitious	__ straightforward	__ persistent
__ assertive	__ dissatisfied	__ practical
__ blunt	__ easy to anger	__ problem-solver
__ competitive	__ goal oriented	__ proud
__ confident	__ impatient	__ pushy
__ courageous	__ inconsiderate	__ sarcastic
__ resolute	__ independent	__ self-starter
__ demanding	__ irritable	__ stubborn
__ determined	__ logical	__ tough

General Characteristics

___ I tend to talk and move at a faster pace than most people around me.

___ At times, I find myself challenging those in authority.

___ I love to set and accomplish goals.

___ I am known to be a great problem-solver.

___ When I notice something that can be improved, I usually voice my opinion or take action and fix it.

___ In conversations, I usually focus on facts vs. emotions.

___ I tend to bring quick decisions.

___ If I want to be honest with myself, I have to admit that *listening* is not one of my main strengths.

___ I dislike repetitive activities.

___ I like to be in charge.

___ I'm a goal-oriented, determined person, who likes challenges and getting down to the bottom-line of things.

___ I like high-speed environments where I can be in control of complete projects.

___ My motto: "Just do it!"

D Style–TOTAL _____

– Fast Paced/People Oriented –

The Influence (I) Behavioral Dimension

Check all that apply to you.

__ compassionate	__ friendly	__ passionate
__ curious	__ fun-loving	__ people-pleaser
__ daydreamer	__ gossipy	__ persuasive
__ disorganized	__ helpful	__ popular
__ easily distracted	__ humorous	__ smiling
__ easygoing	__ impulsive	__ spontaneous
__ entertaining	__ involved	__ talkative
__ enthusiastic	__ optimistic	__ tends to exaggerate
__ excitable	__ outgoing	__ undisciplined
__ forgetful	__ over-promising	__ unsystematic

General Characteristics

___ I tend to talk and move at a faster pace than most people around me.

___ I love to influence others by appealing to logic and emotions.

___ I usually do whatever it takes to stay away from conflict.

___ I tend to see humor in almost any situation.

___ I'm great at starting new projects, but I often jump from task to task and I (often) leave some projects unfinished.

___ I love to make others laugh through my stories, jokes, and funny remarks.

___ I often interrupt others when they speak, with something related or unrelated to the topic at hand.

__ I like to work with people: I care about those around me and I like to help in any way I can vs. working with tasks, numbers, or concepts.

__ I dislike repetitive activities.

__ I have difficulty saying "NO" when others ask for help or favors, even when my time is limited.

__ I like high-speed environments where I can use my verbal skills.

__ I'm a fun-loving, sociable person, who likes to work in teams while I also enjoy entertaining those around me.

__ My motto: "Let's have some fun!"

I Style–TOTAL _____

– Moderate Paced/People Oriented –

The Steadiness (S) Behavioral Dimension

Check all that apply to you.

__ amiable	__ emotional	__ patient
__ calm	__ good listener	__ people pleaser
__ cautious	__ helpful	__ predictable
__ satisfied	__ humble	__ resistant to change
__ conservative	__ indecisive	__ respectful
__ consistent	__ kind	__ sensitive
__ cooperative	__ devoted	__ slow
__ dependable	__ naïve	__ spectator
__ no initiative	__ tactful	__ easily manipulated
__ easygoing	__ passive	__ timid

General Characteristics

__ I tend to talk and move at a moderate pace compared to most people around me.

__ I believe rules were made to be followed.

__ I respect and follow traditions.

__ I don't like to be rushed.

__ I feel really uncomfortable when I have deal with conflict (especially on the job).

__ I have difficulty saying "NO" when others ask for help or favors, even when my time is limited.

__ I don't mind routine tasks.

__ I usually finish what I start.

__ On the job, I like to know exactly what my duties are.

__ I tend not to express my resentments or hurts.

__ I prefer working with people vs. working with tasks, numbers, or concepts.

__ I consider myself a kind, helpful, and sociable person, who likes peace and friendly people.

__ My motto: "Let's all be friends and let's make it work through team effort!"

S Style–TOTAL _____

– Moderate Paced/Task Oriented –

The Conscientiousness (C) Behavioral Dimension

Check all that apply to you.

__ precise	__ distrustful	__ revengeful
__ analytical	__ focused	__ stubborn
__ cautious	__ formal	__ suspicious
__ conscientious	__ hesitant	__ critical
__ conservative	__ introverted	__ methodical
__ consistent	__ organized	__ thorough
__ controlled	__ perfectionist	__ non-emotional
__ dependable	__ predictable	__ unforgiving
__ detail-oriented	__ resentful	__ unfriendly
__ distant	__ resistant to change	__ worrisome

General Characteristics

__ I tend to move and talk at a more moderate pace compared to most people around me.

__ I believe rules were made to be followed.

__ I have high expectations from those around me.

__ I don't like to be rushed.

__ I tend to stay away from risky behaviors and risky/unsafe environments.

__ I like to plan my work and my activities, and I like to stick to the plan as closely as possible.

__ I take pride in my work and I am really good at what I do.

___ On the job, I like to know exactly what my duties are.

___ I don't mind routine/repetitive tasks.

___ I usually finish what I start.

___ It energizes me when I work on my own on tasks, numbers, or concepts vs. working with people.

___ I consider myself to be a highly dependable, analytical, methodical, and detail-oriented person, who enjoys working solo on complex tasks.

___ My motto: "Measure twice, cut once!"

C Style–TOTAL _____

Communication Skills Magic–Step-by-Step Strategies to Improving Your Personal and Professional Relationships, by E.G. Sebastian, Copyright © 2009

Helpful Quick Summary of the Four Styles

This quick summary will help you recognize what personality-communication style your loved one falls into, and how to best work and communicate with them.

Dominance (D)–*fast paced* and *task oriented*
Outspoken and determined, D's are dynamic, goal-oriented people who like to take charge, bring quick decisions, and want quick results.

Influence (I)–*fast paced and people oriented*
Enthusiastic and friendly, I's are outgoing, high-energy people who like to influence others with their wit, humor, and persuasive skills.

Steadiness (S)–*moderate paced* and *people oriented*
Caring and supportive, S's are calm and kind people, who are great at providing support and comfort to others, following rules, listening, and being great team players.

Conscientiousness (C)–*moderate paced* and *task oriented*
Cautious and detail-oriented, C's are focused and dependable people who love to work with tasks and concepts; they like to plan their work and are committed to quality and accuracy in all areas.

How to Defuse Conflict with the Four Styles & What They Expect of You

You have now learned more about yourself and others' personality type and communication style. The best way to utilize the information below is to carefully review it prior to your next family meeting. At that time, adapt it to your own situation, stay open-minded, employ a sense of humor, and realize that practice makes perfect.

When in conflict with a <u>Dominance</u> type family member:

- Run! You can't win. This is a behavioral style that can really *blow the lid off* and will fight like a tiger. <u>Wait till they calm down</u>.

- Let them vent. They will get more upset if you interrupt them.

- When giving your side of the story, stay calm, appeal to their logic, and <u>use brief sentences loaded with</u> facts.

- Do not lose your temper, nor give in to them.

- Use non-emotional language.

When in conflict with an <u>Influence</u> type family member:

- Understand that they do not like conflict.

- Allow them to vent. Listen to their side of the story and then ask them to calm down and discuss the issue calmly.

- Be prepared for emotional outbursts.

- Validate their emotions: "I understand why this makes you upset, but let's take a look at the facts, and let's see how we can come up with a solution."

- Have them repeat what you agreed upon.

When in conflict with a <u>Steadiness</u> type family member:

- Often conflict can go on undetected due to their tendency to hide their negative emotions.

- Encourage them to talk.

- Listen deeply and do not interrupt.

- Understand that they will do everything in their power to defuse the conflict themselves.

- Do not raise your voice.

- Validate their "pain." Suggest working on a solution together.

- They are often unaware of the existence of a conflict. Break it to them in a calm, friendly manner.

When in conflict with a <u>Conscientiousness</u> type family member:

- They often will carry on grudges for months or years without the other person knowing why there is tension between the two.

- Avoid raising your voice.

- Encourage them to open up and speak freely.

- Even if their reasoning sounds unreasonable, validate their emotions. Say, "I'm sorry to hear that *xyz* made you feel that way. Let's try to come up with a solution that will be a win-win for both of us."

- Quote rules and regulations whenever possible.

Communication Skills Magic–Step-by-Step Strategies to Improving Your Personal and Professional Relationships, by E.G. Sebastian, Copyright © 2009

Use Effective & Supportive Behaviors in Family Meetings

Important guidelines to *set* and *abide* by when meeting with your family members in a nutshell:

Create Goal(s)

Set Purpose & Intention
Show Respect & Listen Deeply

Use Discretion & Trust
Show Consideration

Use Acknowledgment & Validation
Give Constructive Feedback

Accept and Share Responsibility with Integrity
Work and Communicate toward the Same Goal

Practice Resolving Issues & Sharing Difficult Feelings by
Creating an 'Opening' for Trust

Behaviors that HELP = Support and Create Trust

- Be on time, prepared, and ready to go,
participate, volunteer to do tasks.

- Listen to understand; speak to be understood.
- Engage in open, honest, and direct communication.
- Value others' opinions and ask questions.
- Create/have an agenda and stick to it.
- Build on others' ideas and insights.
- Be positive/optimistic.
- Critique ideas, not people.
- Perform promised follow-up.
- Pay attention and stay open-minded.
- Take problems seriously.
- Be courteous, honest, and trusting.
- Say what you feel/think.
- Take responsible risks.
- Use "we" expressions and thought more than "I" expressions.
- Support each other in and outside the meeting.
- Show commitment toward making it work.
- Display or engage in a sense of humor.
- Set realistic goals/time frame on goals.
- Appreciate others' skills, abilities, and personality differences.
- Establish clearly-defined roles/guidelines.
- Distribute responsibilities equally.
- Demonstrate positive body language.

> *Nurturing each other along will be much more productive than to criticize one another.*
> *~ Daniela Bumann*

Behaviors that HINDER = **Destroy Trust**

- Showing negative body language, such as falling asleep, sighing, eye-rolling, folded arms, looking down, shaking head "no," and not getting involved
- Showing little or no enthusiasm in order to contribute to the meeting
- Attacking others personally
- Dominating discussion
- Engaging in name calling /stereotyping
- Making guilt-throwing, manipulative statements
- Jumping from one topic to another
- Masking statements as questions
- Agreeing with everything
- Avoiding decision-making or closure
- Interrupting others
- Saying "no" before thinking "yes"
- Expressing futility, resignation, or helplessness
- Sharing opinions without fact
- Taking phone calls within the meeting room
- Reflecting boredom/don't pay attention
- Participating in side conversations
- Talking over each other
- Not listening
- Close-mindedness
- Using "you" statements
- Judging ideas/others

- Doing other distracting work
- "Triangling" outside the meeting
- Cross-talking (between two people that leaves others outside the discussion)
- Sarcastic or caustic remarks
- Going off the agenda and "chasing rabbits"

(Imparts by Deborah Mackin, New Directions Consulting)

> *In humility, you can find tolerance and flexibility to grown, surpassing rigidity of knowing it all.*
> *–Daniela Bumann*

Putting It All Together

Remember, information/tools are only as good as applied. You may have learned something new about yourself or others that surprised you, or even made you laugh about yourself or another. These tools are to support you and make your communications easier and more productive in order to achieve the goal of creating the best solution possible for your loved one.

Above all, keep at heart that your loved one is most likely feeling overwhelmed, struggling with the loss of independence, and adapting to a whole new set of circumstances themselves. That's why together as a family you can achieve more.

Ask for Support

If you find yourself grappling with your emotions, this is the perfect time to see a coach, counselor, or get involved in caregiver support groups. This is an emotional time, and feeling all you do is normal. It's how you cope with your feelings that will make a big difference. I provided you with lots of information, but these are only the basics.

Please reach out for more support on mediation, conflict resolution, coaching, placement, caregiver support groups, etc. and get the help you need. Life is a journey. Remember to breathe through the tough times, and know that you CAN do it!

Final Words

I am very excited to contribute to this book, as I have had a passion to advocate for elders and their caregivers. I have, myself, been an involved caregiver from a "distance" (my loved ones lived in Switzerland) and know the challenges of caregiving and working with my family all too well. When I was invited to contribute, I thought the idea and purpose of the book was genius, and very well-needed indeed. Having become bi-cultural, I have deeply studied diversity, communication/relational styles, positive psychology, etc. and felt blessed to add value to this book. I hope that you find my sharing useful. All information is only as good as applied. Keep it up. I know you can do it!

 **bumann**

"Liberator" Coach & Corporate Consultant

Confidence for Success | Staff Training and Retreats | Conquer and Exceed your Goals!

Are you looking for...
...and more dramatic ways to improve:

- ✓ Focus, Work Performance, and Sales

- ✓ Winner's Mindset & Leadership Skills

- ✓ Employee Wellness & Team Productivity

- ✓ Trainings addressing Skill AND Mindset

- ✓ Custom-tailored Interactive Staff/ Caregiver Retreats to Boost Self-confidence

- ✓ Celebrating Team Accomplishments/ Increasing Momentum Toward New Goals

- ✓ High-Energy Motivational Programs

Daniela is an optimist, passionate entrepreneur, life-time learner, and self-starter since 1993 (immigrated to USA to 1989). She has engaged in the life-long study in the areas of Positive Psychology, Winner's Mindset/Habits and Work-Life Balance Integration Mastery.

Daniela has worked with companies such as Kaiser, Catholic Charities, National Multiples Sclerosis Society, Office on Aging, Desert Oasis Healthcare, Career Colleges of America, Girl Scouts, VNA, National Association for Female Executives, Somerford Place, Inland Caregiver Resources Center, Banks and Social Service fields in Switzerland, to mention a few.

"If you're ready to take your business and life to higher levels and sustain continuous growth and improvement, then you must work with my friend Daniela. She focuses on getting you rapid results by getting you laser-focused, cutting through the clutter, and inspiring you to produce outcomes! And, Daniela comes from the heart and truly cares about making a positive difference in the lives of others!" - **James Malinchak** Featured on ABCs Hit TV Show, "Secret Millionaire" - One of America's Leading Keynote Speakers & Business Coaches

Reach out for your complimentary assessment @ 951.235.8393 TODAY!

VibrantLivingNow.org • Tel: 951.235.8393 • PO Box 214, Redlands, CA 92373 • info@vibrantlivingnow.org

Notes

_____

_____

_____

_____

_____

_____

_____

_____

_____

_____

_____

_____

_____

_____

_____

_____

_____

_____

Notes

25

Taking Care of Yourself through the Caregiving Process

❧

DAVID FRASER
Inland Caregiver Resource Center

Are you a caregiver? If you are like most people, you think of caregivers as people who are paid to help with the care of someone, not someone like you who is not paid. And you probably don't think of yourself as a caregiver first.

You are a wife, husband, daughter, son, brother, sister, relative, or friend, and you happen to help take care of a relative or friend. You are committed to helping because of your relationship and are more defined by your relationship and less as a "caregiver." You may or may not love the person you care for, but you do it anyway–often, at great sacrifice. If you do help a relative or friend to remain independent, or if you help with the things they can't manage themselves, then you are a caregiver. Perhaps you help someone with a physical condition like cardio-pulmonary disease or severe arthritis, or someone who has a condition which effects thinking, memory, and reasoning like Alzheimer's, stroke, Huntington's disease, Parkinson's, or traumatic brain injury. No matter what the cause of the condition, caregiving can be very demanding of your time, energy, and emotional resources.

However you identify yourself, and irrespective of the condition that causes the person for whom you care to need you, you are among a growing throng of Americans that are largely unrecognized and under-appreciated for their efforts. But one thing you should know is that there is help and support. There is help to deal with the whole range of issues confronting you, and there is help to enable you to see the importance of taking care of yourself at this time. Even if you think you have everything under control and you have no sense of being burdened, it would be wise to take stock and plan ahead for when care might become more difficult. In this chapter, we will explore why it is important to get help–and the sooner the better. We'll also look at resources that are available to help you and the person for whom you care.

A Growing Trend

If you are a caregiver, you have plenty of company. Eighty percent of the care of frail or dependent adults is provided by family members or other unpaid (informal) caregivers at home. A Department of Health and Human Service survey in 1998 concluded that there were 52 million informal and family caregivers helping someone 20+ who is chronically ill or disabled, and 34 million adults provide care to adults 50+. Researchers expect these numbers to climb as boomers age and need help themselves. Additionally, 59% to 70% of caregivers are female, making caregiving very much a women's issue. The majority of caregivers are middle-aged (35-65 years old), and a number of studies have shown that between 25% to 35% of the American workforce are currently providing, or have recently provided, care to someone 65 or older. Working and caregiving has its own rigors and demands.

Even after the person receiving care leaves home and goes into a long-term care facility, informal caregiving continues. People continue to visit the dependent person in their facility. Family caregivers take home laundry, assist with feeding, keep a watchful eye on the person's care, and manage their finances and legal affairs. And they continue to worry, feeling stressed and burdened. For many caregivers, sleep loss, juggling multiple demands, taking over responsibilities they've never had, and foregoing their own medical care to ensure that the person receiving care is always put first are common issues of concern.

Caring for an adult may last a year, or it might last 40 years or longer. A 2003 study found that 4.3 years was the average time of providing care. Another study showed that over 40% of caregivers had provided care for five or more years, and nearly one-fifth had been caregiving for ten or more years. Caregiving is time consuming too, with 20% providing more than forty hours per week. Older caregivers (frequently spouses) spend more time providing care–28% of caregivers who provide 40 or more hours a week are over 65. And, as cognitive impairments worsen with Alzheimer's and other dementias, the time spent in caregiving rises.

The Burden Caregivers Carry

Research has uncovered many startling facts about caregiving and caregivers. Nearly two-thirds of caregivers show symptoms of clinical depression. These caregivers may also feel hopeless and helpless, paralyzed in their ability to change their situation. Adding to their problems is their lowered sense of being effective in what they do–a feeling that it doesn't matter how hard they try, they just can't get it all done or get it done right. Some caregivers become very hard and unforgiving of themselves and have incredibly unrealistic expectations. When they connect with a notion that their efforts can somehow miraculously heal or cure the person being cared for, they can become frustrated and overwhelmed.

The caregiver's physical health may also suffer. Caregivers may have increased blood pressure and insulin levels, may have impaired immune systems, and may be at increased risk for cardiovascular disease. Elderly spousal caregivers (66-96 years old) who experience caregiver-related stress have a 63% higher mortality rate than non-caregivers of the same age. In other words, if you are older and caregiving and you haven't gotten your stress under control, you have as great a risk of dying from the stress and strain of caregiving as a smoker dying of a smoking-related disease.

Caregiving can cause many types of problems resulting from the stress and strain of caregiving. We just touched on the most common and well-researched. Two other issues need to be discussed before moving on to discuss how and where to turn for help.

Until recently, grief and loss and something called "ambiguous loss" have received less attention in the literature on caregiving.

Most everyone knows that grief is a natural process, a universal experience to profound loss. Grief is usually associated with the death of a loved one and is characterized by a deep sadness, a sense of shock, and even disorientation. An inability to focus and short-term memory problems are also common. And, most everyone knows that there are stages of grief which are not necessarily passed through in a consistent order–denial, anger, bargaining, depression, and acceptance. Within these general stages, a person in grief may also experience shock, emotional swings, feelings of panic, and isolation.

What does grief have to do with caregiving? Both the caregiver and the care receiver have much to grieve. The care receiver, even with a dementing disorder, is aware that they have lost their independence, lost physical abilities they once had, lost their ability to be a productive member of the household and, in the case of dementia patients, lost their memory. The caregiver is a witness to these losses and grieves for the care receiver's losses and their own. The caregiver has lost, to a greater or lesser degree, their freedom as their lives become more dedicated to taking care of someone else. The caregiver may have had to give up their job to do full-time caregiving. The loss of friends and increasing isolation brought on by the demands of caregiving is another loss. Caregivers may experience a loss of hope and meaning in life, leaving them bereft and lost.

Grief provokes a host of physical and emotional symptoms including low energy, disruptions in sleep patterns (sleeping all the time or losing sleep), and changes in eating patterns. Difficulty concentrating or following through on tasks, irritability, wailing rages, or passive resignation to everything are not uncommon. With both the caregiver and care receiver experiencing some level of grief throughout the long process of caregiving, neither has much in the way of emotional resources to lend to the other. Outside help and support is essential. Having friends, relatives, pastors, rabbis, or community professionals who understand grief and who can listen and offer solace, hope, and practical suggestions to help get the caregiver through their deepest times of grieving is very important. Understanding grief and getting more understanding about the grieving process through books or articles, poetry, or inspirational books can also help guide the caregiver through their grief.

Understanding that the caregiver's grief is different from the loss of a loved one through death–it is a long-term process of witnessing a gradual decline or it might be a series of losses experienced in numerous crises over a period of years. Caregivers will often continually cycle through the various stages of grief throughout the whole period of their caregiving until they come to the end with the death of the person they care for. During this time, they may find themselves longing for the death of the patient so that the patient might be relieved of their pain and suffering, but also so that it would bring an end to the caregiver's own suffering. Inevitably, these thoughts can produce more guilt for caregivers. Participating in a support group or educational classes with other caregivers can be a great help as you can share with other caregivers who experience these kinds of thoughts and know that you are not selfish or evil–you are going through a tough time under tough circumstances and it is natural for you to have these thoughts and feelings. Normalizing this experience can help to alleviate much of the suffering–but not all.

Caregiving for someone who has sustained brain damage as a result of an accident or illness has more complicated grieving issues associated with it. As mentioned above, the pattern/staging of grief for these caregivers is different. They rarely get to the final stage of acceptance. The issues and concerns are so different that a re-examination of the helpfulness of the grief/loss model has begun to occur. Pauline Boss, a researcher, writer, and professor who has worked with families of head injury survivors and those with Alzheimer's disease has written extensively and brought to the table a discussion about "ambiguous loss."

In her book, *Ambiguous Loss,* and her more recent book, *Loss, Trauma, and Resilience*, Dr. Boss describes the difference between ordinary loss/grief and ambiguous loss. She also discusses the differences in helping people cope with ambiguous loss. She states that ambiguous loss differs from ordinary loss in that there is no verification of death or no certainty that the person will come back or return to the way they used to be. People who have brain damage and resulting cognitive problems, changes in personality, and a severe reduction in their capacity to be independent become different people. The person they once were is gone. The mental/ emotional person is lost but the physical person is still there. This is the source of the ambiguity experienced by those closest to them. This ambiguity–a sense of disorientation with normal reality challenged–creates a cascade of feelings and concerns. Constant sorrow, feelings of being immobilized, doubt, confusion, a loss of self-efficacy, anxiety, helplessness, and conflict are just a few.

"Ambiguous loss freezes the grief process and prevents closure, paralyzing couples and family functioning," Boss states. The challenge then becomes how to get out. As Boss' work has gained recognition, more agency personnel are devising educational programs and creating new types of support groups and other services which help caregivers cope with this aspect of caregiving. The critical tasks for caregivers to cope with ambiguous loss includes the following: 1) Finding Meaning; 2) Tempering Mastery; 3) Reconstructing Identity; 4) Normalizing Ambivalence; 5) Revising Attachment; and 6) Rediscovering Hope. While this seems like a very ambitious approach, there are in fact a set of down-to- earth and practical steps a caregiver can take to change their thinking and their behaviors to cope with ambiguous loss. However, the key to moving beyond the paralysis of ambiguous loss to rediscovering hope and meaning is getting involved with an educational program, support group, life coach, or therapist. It requires reaching out for help.

The Reward

Caregiving is not all doom and gloom, however. Many caregivers find rich satisfaction in being able to help a disabled relative or friend. Many find that the relationship they have with the person they care for involves more physical touching and an emotional closeness that may not have existed for a long time before–if ever. An appreciation of the wonder of the gift of life, of grace found in small ways, and the power of love to overcome all can be among the blessings of caregiving. Caregivers may also find great satisfaction in being able to meet the challenges of caregiving and to learn to appreciate themselves and the gifts and abilities they bring into this relationship.

Support for Caregivers

Caregivers are often reluctant to ask for help. This is odd because at least a third of caregivers say they don't get as much help as they need and don't get as much relief from their caregiving as they would like. Pride, difficulty accepting help from strangers, not wanting to upset the person they care for by bringing in a stranger, and viewing assistance from non-profit agencies or public (city and county entities) as a form of welfare keep caregivers from asking for help. Those who do seek help encounter a system that is a fragmented maze of services with complicated rules and regulations regarding eligibility. It is not uncommon for caregivers to start the day by calling one agency and getting referred to another and then another and so on until the end of the day when they are referred back to the agency with which they started. At that point, they scream in exasperation and give up. Who wouldn't?

While there are many similarities among caregivers, it is vitally important to recognize that each caregiver is unique. It is helpful to find commonalities with other caregivers, but the bottom line is that your walk through the valley of caregiving is lonely because it is so unique to your situation. Advice gleaned from books or articles and even tips and suggestions offered by friends or professionals always have to be filtered through the prism of your experience and knowledge. Caregivers can become so desperate that they'll try anything and then if it doesn't work, they'll just give up trying to change their situation. This is tough work–no one solution works for all. But you must remember you have solved many other problems in your life, you have developed the strength and resources to get through other tough times, and you will manage this one–hopefully with lots of help from others.

Caregivers who are successful in finding help for themselves and for the person they care for are dogged in their pursuit and learn some simple tricks to get through the maze. While this effort is taxing and frustrating, the risks of going it alone as a caregiver are far greater. We'll take a look at how one can reduce the pain of this process.

First however, if you find yourself resisting help from anyone, take an honest look at your reasons. If you are losing sleep or feeling anxious or overwhelmed at any time because of your caregiving responsibilities, look for help. If you are so convinced that no one can take care of your loved one like you can and you are exhausted in the process, look for help. All caregivers need to get beyond the belief that they can do it all alone. Get help to look at how and why you resist getting help.

Strategies to Make It Easier

Let's turn now to what you can do to get help and look at some strategies to better take care of yourself. First let's look at a strategy that can be helpful as you search for the help you need.

1. Identify Your Needs

Get a notebook or three-ring binder to make notes.

- Start by making a list of the problems the person you care for has, then a list of the problems you are encountering in their care.

- Note physical or health issues and concerns, behaviors that trouble you, and questions you have about diagnosis or prognosis.

  - Is the behavior you're seeing in the other normal for their condition?

  - What bugs you?

  - How are your financial resources?

  - Do you get a break (respite) from providing care?

  - Have you lost contact with other family members or friends because of the demands of caring leaving you isolated?

Once you've created this list, go through it to pick out the issues or concerns that are most important to you right now.

Keep this list handy when you begin to look for help so that you can shape your search around the things that are important to you.

2. Create a System

As you get ready to surf the Internet or start making calls, create a system in your notebook for jotting down websites visited that you can return to and agencies that you call.

- For your agency contacts, note the date, the name of the person you spoke with, and a brief summary of what they said they would do for you. Will they contact you by mail or phone?

- Write down any assignments or instructions for follow-up that they give you; and also note the names of agencies, contacts and phone numbers they provide for you to follow-up with.

- If you need to call the agency or service provider back, ask for the person you last talked with so you don't have to go through your story all over again.

- Be prepared to provide personal information, but do not give out your social security number or other highly sensitive information over the phone. Be sure you can trust the agency first before you provide this kind of information.

3. Search for Resources

If you have access to the Internet, you can start by searching "caregiving." You'll find plenty of resources.

- Family Caregiver Alliance, one of California's Caregiver Resource Centers and host of the National Center on Caregiving, has a great website www.caregiver.org. This is a good place to start for a wide range of information and resources on caregiving.

  - www.networkofcare.org provides information on elder care resources in several states including California and Oregon.

- The federal government's Administration on Aging provides information on the Family Caregiver Support Program through their website www.aoa.gov.

- If you begin to search for resources or information by telephone, 211 will connect you to an information and referral service in your area in California.

- Many areas have a Volunteer Center or a United Way that can direct you to specialized information and referral services.

- You can often turn to your local "Area Agency on Aging" for information and assistance. Try looking them up in the phone book (try under county agencies) or call a local senior center in your area and they should be able to direct you to a help line.

- You can also search online or by phone for disease-specific organizations like the Alzheimer's Association, National Parkinson's Foundation, Multiple Sclerosis Society, Huntington's Disease Society of America, American Cancer Society, American Heart Association (for heart disease and strokes), and many more.

- Information about the disease or condition you are dealing with and information about community resources can be very helpful. Numerous "fact sheets" are available on any number of caregiving topics.

- Visit your local library and get help from a librarian to find books and other resources to educate yourself. Lack of knowledge is a common concern for caregivers but there is information available.

- Many organizations provide training and education classes for caregivers. These can be very helpful.

- Caregiver-specific organizations in your community or those funded through the Area Agency on Aging and the Family Caregiver Support Program are good starting points as well. If you are lucky in your calling, you'll find an information and referral specialist who can listen to your issues and concerns and direct you to the most appropriate community resources. Community resources can be roughly divided into public (government funded) agencies, non-profit agencies and faith-based organizations. The kinds of resources that commonly are available to caregivers include:

  - support groups (frequently disease-specific, e.g., Alzheimer's support groups)

  - case management or care planning services

  - adult day care centers

  - private duty home health agencies which can provide respite care

  - registries for home care workers

  - diagnostic centers and specialized treatment centers

  - agencies that provide financial assistance for a variety of concerns

  - legal resources (legal aid, elder law attorneys, Medicaid/Medi-Cal planning specialists, etc.)

  - resources that can help you find long-term care placement facilities (assisted living or nursing homes)

4. Take Care of Yourself

Once you begin to look for help, you are already on the road to taking better care of yourself.

- The place where self-care really starts is in making and keeping your own doctor's appointments. This should include regular physical checkups and lab tests for your age group. For women, breast exams and regular gynecological check-ups are extremely important and should not be put off.

- Don't neglect your mental or emotional health either.

- Find people who really listen and understand. Join a support group.

  - See a therapist or life coach.

  - Think about maintaining a life apart from your life as a caregiver.

  - Reach out to friends who support you and care for you, and make plans to do things with them.

  - This means finding a way to get away from time to time. Get help from other family members to relieve you or contact an agency that assists with respite care to get a break from caregiving.

- Find time for fun activities–arts and crafts projects, yoga classes, choral groups, Bible study–activities you really enjoy and ones you can do with others. That way, you deal with your need for other human contact and fellowship and engage in fun activities.

- Find ways to relieve your stress.

  - Pray or meditate.

  - Relax in a hot bath.

- Read a good book.

- Listen to soothing music.

- Exercise. Physical exercise can be helpful
  to relieve stress, boost energy levels.
  and improve your sense of well-being.
  Take a walk, or do some yoga (even in
  a chair) or ride a stationary bike.

- Learn the art of patience and compassion. There will always be good days and bad days.

- Learn to communicate effectively with the person you care for without laying blame.

- Make sure you get plenty of opportunities to laugh and get your daily quotient of hugs. No one formula or prescription for self-care works for all. There will need to be a lot of trial and error to find what works for you; but, with persistence, you will find a way.

- Lastly, it is so important that you learn to lighten up on yourself. We can be so harsh and judgmental towards ourselves when compassion and forgiveness are really what is needed.

5. Perspective

To survive caregiving, one needs to let go of perfection and the need to master every problem and situation. One must learn that one's best effort is often good enough. Caregivers who learn that keeping an immaculate house, cooking three meals each day, and doing everything just so is not possible or realistic experience less stress, burden, and guilt. They learn to adjust and adapt. Caregiving is a course in adaptation and finding the inner resources to build resilience–the ability to keep on going by making adjustments and having the flexibility to try new approaches. Caregiving can teach great compassion for the person you care for. It can also teach you how to treat yourself as kindly and offer to yourself the degree of forgiveness that you extend to your loved one. Self-care and compassion for your own suffering can be one of the great blessings of caregiving, but it requires that you pay attention and work intentionally to change old habits and learn new ones. There is help in the community to enable you to tackle this most important task in caregiving. Ask for the support you need. There are good people ready to help you.

"Helping Families and the Community Cope with and Manage the Challenges of Caregiving"

1430 East Cooley Drive, Suite 240
Colton, CA 92324
(800) 675-6694

www.inlandcaregivers.org

Follow us on Facebook

https://www.inlandcaregivers.com/#

Family Caregiver Services
- Information and Referral
- Respite - A Break from Caregiving
- Short Term Counseling
- Trainings/Classes on Caregiving
- Ongoing Case Management
- Support Groups
- Community Based Occupational Therapy Program

Senior Support Services
- Information and Referral
- Homemaker Services
- Personal Care Services
- Adult Day Care
- Minor Home Repairs
- Program to Encourage Active and Rewarding Lives

Please note services vary by county and depending on funding available

Notes

Final Note to the Baby Boomer

DARLENE MERKLER

I hope you have found this book helpful in providing outstanding care for your parent. My goal was to give you a book in which you could find resources for your specific needs and record all of the information pertinent to their care. I wanted you to feel comforted and sure that you have all of the information you need, and that you could relax if for any reason someone had to take over your caregiving role.

Most importantly, I wanted you to be reminded that you must take care of yourself in order to continue providing excellent care for your loved ones. You have one of the most rewarding and exhausting jobs an adult could take on, particularly if you have to do so in addition to another career and other family obligations. Please, for your sake, and for your loved one's sake, take care of yourself physically, mentally, and emotionally. Ask for the support you need. Enjoy the time you have with your loved one.

May you be blessed for your willingness and efforts to give your loved one the best possible care so that their days, though numbered, can be comfortable and happy!

Notes

_____

_____

_____

_____

_____

_____

_____

_____

_____

_____

_____

_____

_____

_____

_____

_____

_____

Made in the USA
San Bernardino, CA
20 January 2020